STRONG ENOUGH TO CRY

DISCOVER THE NEW KIND OF WARRIOR
WITHIN AND BECOME UNSTOPPABLE

ERICA ORMSBY

ISBN: 9781950621101 (ebook)

ISBN: 978-1-950621-15-6 (paperback)

Brad, my love, I am eternally grateful for the massive space you've held for all of me. I love you more:)
Thank you for your courage.

CONTENTS

THE PROBLEM WITH TRYING TO AVOID
UNCOMFORTABLE EMOTIONS
IS THAT EMOTIONS ARE INHERENTLY
UNAVOIDABLE
INTERWOVEN THROUGHOUT
THE HUMAN EXPERIENCE
TO RUN FROM OR SUPPRESS THEM
IS NOT ONLY FUTILE
BUT TETHERS US TO THEM.
TO HAVE THE COURAGE
TO TURN AND FACE,
FEEL ALL THAT WE FEEL
AND NOT RUN
IS A GREAT ACT OF COURAGE.
IT IS HERE WE FIND PEACE
WARRIORS WHO ARE STRONG ENOUGH TO CRY.

- ERICA ORMSBY

1

Run.

1

RUN.

For some reason, I was running a little bit late to PE that day. As a second-grader, who knows why maybe because I was just taking forever or needed to use the bathroom. I was probably just dinking around - like a second-grader. Either way, I was running late. I ran across the huge green field where we played during recess. I'd had all of my adventures with friends and met for PE class there. I would do a variety of fun shenanigans depending on what the teacher had come up with for that day. Even from a distance, I could see all of the kids in my second-grade class as I ran toward them. A couple of kids were lined up against the fence, the rest were in two lines spanning out from each side of my PE teacher facing them. As I closed the gap, my excitement and curiosity rose.

When my teacher could see me, she pointed and motioned for me to go to the fence next to the now, one-child, still standing there. I was out of breath as we faced our classmates standing in their two lines. I thought, *What is this? How fun!* My teacher said, "OK, we have two more to go. Who wants Sara on their team?" The kids began excitedly arguing over who would get to have Sarah on their team. It went back-and-forth for a few seconds until the teacher said, "OK! Sarah, you're going on John's team and Erica, you're going on Amber's." Just as she finished saying this both groups began arguing about not wanting me on their team.

They were yelling over each other saying, "That's not fair!" "We don't want Erica, we don't want her on our team!" It suddenly became really hard to breathe. I felt like I was shrinking. My eyes kept darting back-and-forth watching as my classmates argued over who *had to have me* on their team. I didn't understand at the time how much that moment would affect me throughout my life moving forward. I remember becoming so embarrassed, sad, humiliated, and even afraid. *I wanted to run.* Runaway from the circumstance, and run away from the overwhelming feelings I had inside. Frankly, if there would have been a fast-forward button, I would have frantically pushed it. I wanted to just avoid everything about what had just happened altogether. But there was no fast-forward button to push.

Instead, my teacher tried her best to make a firm decision that I would be on Amber's team and that we needed to get the game started. It's a blur in my mind what happened next. I just know that I played the rest of the game and that I felt feelings that I could not explain, nor did I know what to do with and they felt awful. So I did the only thing I could think of- stuff them down and begin building a wall. I wanted to cry.

My eyes were burning but then with fury inside of me, I decided that *I would never let them see me cry*. I became angry. A rookie master of disguise, I turned my pain into anger, but I know it showed. It wasn't a conscious decision to choose anger over what I was really feeling. But the anger gave me a sense of self-protection. I can't say that was the first time I had felt rejection, shame, or humiliation but I can tell you that's the first time I can remember being aware that I refused to let myself feel how I was feeling. I'm glad I didn't know then that it absolutely wouldn't be the last time.

This book isn't about digging up what happened in the past to ponder our crappiest memories. It's a deep dive into what the hell to do with all of the crappy feelings that come up during these moments in life. Further, to gain a whole new understanding of how to harness the actual power of your own emotions. Why? In short, avoiding our uncomfortable emotions holds us back from fully living. Stuffing them down and locking them away may seem like a viable option but I assure you, it's not the option with the happy ending we are attempting to achieve in the first place. As we move forward, you'll be able to tap into a *new kind of warrior within*.

And don't worry I'm not going to tell you that you need to become like a Zen peaceful monk! But you do need to become a badass at navigating your own internal emotions because the alternative is to have them shape your life in ways, I guarantee, you never wanted. In my first book, I Am. Happy. Healthy. Free. I laid a lot of track on how to think differently so we're not stuck. The feedback I received was great except for this one question that I was continually asked that let me know I needed to cover some more ground. People kept asking, "How are you happy all the time?" And I was like, "Whaaat?! Oh no no no, there is a serious point that has been missed. I am far from happy all the time and that's ironically part of being happy." The confused, semi-discouraged looks I received back gave me the courage to explain.

The pain at the pit of my stomach makes it hard to take a full breath. As my mind is racing for reasons to explain why I am so upset. I find myself going down a long, dark rabbit hole of blame and more anger. I want to make these overwhelming feelings stop – as fast as I possibly can. I need a solution, a distraction. I need to get as far from feeling like this as possible. I want to run. --I wrote this in my journal when I was upset-on a random Tuesday.

This is normal (if we can even use the word normal anymore). Truly. We FEEL often. When we feel uncomfortable, we tend to feel like getting comfortable as quickly as possible. I hated feeling all shadowy feelings. You might be thinking, doesn't everybody? No shit. No one wants to feel rejection, sadness, anger, insecurity, panic, frustration, betrayal, devastation, jealousy, guilt, shame, pain... but we do because we are human.

We are terrified by all of these emotions and we will do crazy things to get away from them. I think many of us avoid bad feelings like the plague. I'll speak for myself: I feel like I have a volcano inside of me sometimes. Chest burning, tight stomach, tight throat-occasionally a headache for good measure. I am a deep thinker but most of what I feel used to be too much for me. I was terrified of how I felt. When I was younger my feelings felt like they might eat me alive. When I was older-same.

I just got even better at hiding them, from myself and others. I wanted to *feel* tough as nails. I even gravitated dominantly toward male friends because males had been more conditioned to stuff emotions than females and that was more comfortable for me. As pain levels rose, my anger rose and many times turned to rage. Being more of an implode-er than an explode-er, I would become more self-destructive. When I was really young, it looked like drugs, alcohol, looking perfect, people-pleasing, and bad relationships. When I got older, it looked like serious overachievement, some alcohol, trying to be perfect, people-pleasing, and bad relationships. I felt so complicated inside and overwhelmed by myself. I just did everything I could to suppress, avoid, numb, sidestep, distract, you name it, to not have to feel all the crap.

No matter what I did or how fast I ran, there I was with everything trapped inside. I didn't know how to let myself feel what was inside of me without wanting to self-destruct. Couldn't I just ignore how I felt inside and, eventually, the feelings would just go away? No. I found that time does not heal emotions. They patiently or impatiently wait until they are expressed.

Ironically, they seem to really petrify with time. Maybe what started as a feeling of anger one day, left unacknowledged, becomes an angry person over time. I would feel any given uncomfortable emotion, then I would ignore it, and when I felt it again, it's almost as if it would compress it into something even deeper and over time even bigger. Like adding pieces of clay to a ball. Eventually, the ball can become enormous. I don't claim to be a psych-expert. However, I have had my share of massive emotional roadblocks that kept me stuck on repeat for a very long time and I broke free. I feel compelled to share how with others. I eventually learned the power and importance of being able to feel what I'm feeling and navigate forward. The result has been living fully and never feeling trapped. That may not make perfect sense right now "feel what I'm feeling" but I can assure you, as you read on, it's my hope that a clear path of how to go from stuck to unstuck will unfold.

I used to equate emotions with weakness. There's so much built into our culture that says so. How many times have we heard in the movies or stories or from personal experience inside our homes or at school that emotions are for the weak?

- *Crying is for babies.*
- *Men don't cry.*
- *Don't be so emotional.*
- *You're not going to cry are you?*
- *Don't get emotional, this is business.*

And there are far more derogatory and sexist judgments around people having feelings that I won't write but if you've lived on earth for more than 10 years- you've heard most of them. For centuries, women were portrayed as a weaker gender and feelings seem to be reserved for only women to have. Further, the narrative is slowly changing but historically has gone something like, "Women have emotions because they are not strong like men and weaker so therefore, they have these emotions".

I recently watched an episode of The Amazing Race. A young couple in their mid-twenties were arguing in the back seat of a cab. The guy said, "I'm a soldier, not a woman" -in response to her being upset. Think of the many heroic archetypes that were presented to us for centuries depicting the strongest of the strong, as people who expressed very little, if any, emotion. The only emotion that are uncomfortable that seem to have made the cut in the societal depiction of strength that we are allowed to express without being considered a weak person- is anger. Anger, although uncomfortable, is the "if you aren't happy or stoic- you can be angry, and we won't think you're a total wussy" go-to emotion.

So who cares? Who cares if we are willing to feel our feelings or not? I mean how important can it really be? Our heroes didn't have them, and they came out on top. We want to be strong, not weak.

But what if suppressing our emotions in real life- not in the movies and legends-actually makes us weak.

There are several relentless problems with wanting to avoid uncomfortable emotions at all costs. Well, the first problem is that, as a human being, whether you're male or female, you have every emotion throughout your life from birth until the day you die. Obviously, there are a few exceptions but the vast majority, we all have them ALL. Ironically, having feelings is completely unavoidable and the very act of avoidance tethers us to them. Further, according to the research by Brene Brown and others, we can't really feel all the comfortable emotions- the "good" emotions- when we are suppressing the "bad" ones. In this crazy way, it has become clear that *part of being happy is the willingness to be sad.* How interesting, the very things we want to avoid and run from are, in reality, entirely unavoidable. *The only way out is to stop running.* But if you're anything like me, especially if you had extremely painful emotions or a lifetime of running, making the decision to consider *feeling how you feel* can 100% seem paralyzing or even ridiculous.

Making the decision to face the way that I feel and learning how to navigate the things that I've been avoiding for so long has given me an entirely new level of fulfillment, peace, and the power to create my own destiny. I used to pride myself on how strong I was, and I was strong but I'm even stronger now. I measure it differently today. I used to measure how strong I was by how much I could take and withstand without acknowledging it or "let it get to me". I didn't think about it like that necessarily because that would've required me sitting and feeling how bad I really felt. I just had this "shake it off and get back up" mentality- kind of like a war hero in my mind thinking no matter how much I'm bleeding, no matter how injured I am, I'm strong because I won't let myself acknowledge the pain. I'll just keep moving forward. Sounds badass right? To break through brick walls unscathed.

Everything I've seen about strong and victorious people has showcased their ability to go through any adversity and come out on the other side. What I hadn't taken into account is that my wounds never really seemed to heal, and my life was spent managing the pain in the only way that I understood which was to avoid it altogether. God forbid when unwanted feeling boiled over and I couldn't drink them away, fight them away, achieve them away, spend them away, eat them away --you name it-- and I cried-- I just felt more ashamed followed by more anger.

I was perfectly accustomed to avoiding my feelings at all cost and I truly didn't feel like there was anything wrong with it-- I think deep down, I saw myself as some type of warrior. I got to a place where I made it a point *never to cry*. I told myself that I had gone through so much and survived--nothing and no one would ever break me and by break me, I mean, make me cry. I wouldn't even cry alone where no one would ever know because I refused to feel weak. I'd become a survivor and in my pursuit of survival and strength, I built thick walls so no one could hurt me.

Of course, people could still hurt me and, of course, every time I was rejected, betrayed, or I failed at something it hurt. Really, all those thick walls did was make damn sure I didn't let anybody get too close or vice versa. Remember as a child in class when we were learning about navigating all of the emotions that come up as a human being and how to harness their power for the greater good for ourselves and others? Oh my gosh, of course you don't remember-- I don't either because that class or anything like it didn't exist! Again, if every human being experiences the full spectrum of emotions but does not allow themselves to acknowledge the uncomfortable ones and by that act alone diminishes their ability to feel the good emotions-then what life are we living? If we are caught feeling, we shame ourselves and others... We can see the equation on the wall. Something is really off with this logic. We can't really be happy because we refuse to feel sad.

Feel
Your
Feelings

Can you remember a time in your youth when
you "stuffed away" your emotions?
What was the experience?
Why did you feel you couldn't express them?

_____

_____

_____

_____

_____

_____

_____

_____

_____

_____

_____

_____

The Cost Is Too High

2

THE COST IS TOO HIGH

I t was mid-afternoon on a weekday when I gave away my seven-figure company and everything I had worked for, for the seven years prior. I technically sold my company, but it was for a price so far below its value that in my heart, I will always feel like I gave it away. Did I do this because I am a generous person and just wanted to bless a family with a seven-figure company? Did I do this because I didn't love the company that I had built along with my team? Did I do this because my family and I had plenty of money and plenty of other opportunities and keeping the company just wasn't necessary?

No. The hard and true answer is no to all of the above. Ultimately, I made this decision because I didn't know how to handle the feelings of pain, shame, and anger inside of me and I wanted the feelings to stop. I tried to run from how I felt and couldn't see a way forward, so I let go. I sat in my living room in the big chair facing the soon to be new owners of my company. I had actually made them partners six months prior for similar reasons. We had been through a lot together. Primarily the wife and me. She had trusted and shared my vision for the company working for me and alongside me, through thick and thin.

While building the company, I had also been a single mom with a baby, went through a marriage and divorce, and overcame a battle with alcoholism. (One of the most devastating biological and psychological ways I had attempted to avoid pain). But this decision I made possibly cost me the most. I will admit that deep down there was a part of me that felt I had climbed up the wrong mountain because I had hit fairly significant levels of success at this point but still felt terribly unfulfilled.

I had a nagging sense that there was more for me to do on this earth beyond running that particular company. It turns out there was a lot more. Regardless, I didn't make that decision from an empowered place. I made it while engulfed in fear and shame and a profound sense of unworthiness. I believed that because I struggled so deeply that I didn't deserve the company that I had created. Further, when my former partners approached me, it was with the offer to buy them out or they buy me out. Either way, they didn't want to continue the partnership.

The little girl standing on the field with everyone fighting over who didn't want me on their team--the feelings came up like a monsoon. I felt myself getting smaller and smaller, the panic, the humiliation, the rejection, the pain. So crazy to say it out loud but I thought if I sold them the company, they would still be my friends. Setting judgment aside because, believe me, I judged myself have to death over this, I literally made the decision as a second-grader based on the motives of a child who didn't want to be left. In the moment, I couldn't see any of that, all I could feel was an insurmountable surge of pain and I made a decision as quickly as possible to make it stop. At the time, I didn't have the ability to sit and feel what I was feeling long enough to make a decision from an empowered place.

Between second-grade to this crossroads in my living room, I had a pretty thick portfolio of experiences filled with uncomfortable feelings that were met with my own iron fist for fear that I would be broken if I acknowledged the pain sincerely.

I remember the first time I said I love you to a guy. I was young and so was he, but I meant it with all of my heart. I can still see the sadness in his eyes as he stared back at me in silence until he was finally able to, almost in a whisper, say, "I'm so sorry Erica, I don't love you." I stayed home from school for two days filled with so many emotions that I couldn't seem to express. When I finally got the courage to go back to school, I did my hair as nicely as I could, I put on one of my best outfits because I was going to keep moving forward. I also put on my best game-face. It was maybe 30 minutes into the first period when I discovered that he and one of my closest friends had already become a couple. It doesn't matter how old or young you are, feelings are feelings, and pain is pain, it's not felt any less. All the feelings-- the extremely uncomfortable ones-- surged through me but I pushed them down. When my friend asked me if it was OK that they were together? I said "Sure. I'm over it. I'm glad you're happy." We stayed friends and I never mentioned it again. I was strong and I wasn't going to let them see me cry. In fact, I just wasn't going to cry at all.

These are just a few of many moments in my life where I had so much emotion that I didn't know what to do with but if I keep writing these stories I'll take up the whole book instead of letting you know the magic that happened inside of me later that really set me free.

Back to the moment in my living room, the afternoon where I basically said *OK, yeah, it's fine. I'm fine. I'm happy you're happy.* I already had amassed so many experiences of extremely uncomfortable feelings from rejection, failure, embarrassment- this moment may have just slipped right in with the rest of them but the repercussions cost me so much it was like God in his infinite wisdom- the universe providing the perfect shit storm to force me or eh-hem, give me the profound opportunity to learn how to face all of my emotions and not push them away.

As soon as the papers were signed, we hardly spoke again. She lent me a hair tie in a random yoga class once and we said a brief hello at a soccer game where our kids played in a tournament. The community that I found my identity in, that I loved and felt so connected too--I was no longer welcome. Basically, the life, the friends, and the profession that I had cultivated for almost 15 years vanished. They did not want me on their team. It broke my heart. *This was the beginning of me being strong enough to cry.*

Nearly every man I have ever loved had cheated on me except for my husband, Brad. I had made it through multiple sexual assaults. I had felt pain levels in my past that made taking my own life seem like a reasonable option. But nothing hurt me more than giving away my company or the level of rejection following it.

I signed papers that stated I would no longer do for a living what I had been doing for a living for the last 15 years. I had put my actual blood, sweat, and tears into bringing this company to life and the team that supported it. I gave up my financial freedom and felt the rejection of every person that walked away.

I was going to need to start from scratch again. But this time, I would do it very differently.

I wanted to run so badly.

I had a choice.

Run or Feel.

I chose to feel.

I let ALL my stuff come up.

Every worst fear, insecurity, unworthiness, rejection on steroids - ALL MY SHIT CAME UP.

———

We can run but we can't hide-- how we feel comes up and how we *handle* how we feel makes all the difference in the world. Life has a way of evolving us whether we consciously desire it to or not. There's a new opportunity to be free - integrate the feelings- not suppress them- and evolve in every moment. But when you don't know that - it just feels like the world is coming down around you. Some of us might spend our whole life fighting against life. Some of us might go with the flow, ride the river of life without much resistance, and some of us might really need to understand how the hell this all works before we're willing to let our guard down based on an informed decision. I knew how I was dealing with a lot of my life needed to change. But being the "strong" person that I was- agh- I had a huge pile-up of emotion.

I really am someone that has to understand things inside a very pragmatic framework. Logical and grounded. I wasn't just going to "feel my feelings" unless it truly made sense too. I decided to take a year, to dig in and deal. Now that I had all of the time in the world and just a few friends...I had a blank canvas. I wanted to create something new. Inside and out. It took an explosion for me to see the diamonds in the rubble. I needed this time. It was wild that it took me practically leveling my life to not be distracted.

There's always subtle cues early on before something has to get so loud that you can't focus on anything else but changing that loud noise. I've been heavily invested in personal development, so to speak, since I was in my mid-teens. Following a breaking point at 17, I have been open to making sense of why I did the things I did or understanding events and reactions of my past, which is useful. This has given me greater insight and compassion for myself and others.

However, no matter how much I would analyze my past- it didn't absolve me from needing to learn how to navigate uncomfortable emotions in my present. *Sensemaking and analyzing my past feelings, actions, circumstances, is completely different than understanding and developing this skill of dealing with emotions that come up every day in your present life in real-time.* I had spent a significant amount of time trying to understand my life and other people's lives through counseling, books, workshops, conferences, spirituality, etc. Still, I would seem to continue to have more and more crappy experiences to add to my list of crappy experiences as each year went on.

It became really confusing when the more successful I became and the more money I made, my stress level continued to increase. The part of me that was in a perpetual open sprint away from how I felt each day, wasn't slowing down. As new problems would arise, I might take action to handle the logistics of the problem, but I would make sure I didn't feel the pain of the problem. There are so many creative ways to avoid how you feel at least temporarily. There are the obvious rough ones that we tend to get really judge-y about like alcohol, pills, and drugs, overspending, food, and _____. Then there are these really crafty ways to attempt to not feel what we feel that either fly under the radar or we can even be rewarded for such as high achievement, working constantly, or helping others at the cost of helping ourselves.

Personally I've tested them all and none of them made me feel better for longer than a few hours at a time. Maybe a day if I was lucky. In fact, I noticed a correlation looking back - the harder and faster I'd run, the higher the price I would pay. It was like the more I stopped my emotions, the more exhausted I became. My hyper-productivity caused a perpetual state of exhaustion. Physically, emotionally, and spiritually I could feel myself slipping further and further into disconnect and isolation.

It takes courage to stop running from how you feel. I realized that my perception of letting myself feel uncomfortable emotions was wrong. Feeling was never the weakness I had once believed it to be. It makes sense that if I was going to be potentially really hurt by someone that I would want to protect myself. The further-reaching issue became a generalized fear that I could be hurt just around every corner. I noticed when I was the most vulnerable, I had sustained the most painful wounds. The answer was never to become less vulnerable. It was to become someone who didn't need to run from what's inside them.

I knew through the experience of giving away my company and the pain of that level of rejection that I had to go through it differently this time. The stakes were too high. I had already come so far. I had a son that I not only needed to take care of but really show up in life for him. If I wanted to have healthy relationships and wake up every morning into a career that I love, then I was going to have to feel what I was feeling and stop running. Some part of me knew that before I made any more major decisions I would have to wait until I felt strong enough to cry.

There was a point where I stopped asking why and I started asking what now?

Feel
Your
Feelings

As an adult, have you ever made an emotion-based decision that you regret?
What positives came out of that experience?

_____

_____

_____

_____

_____

_____

_____

_____

_____

_____

_____

_____

_____

_____

Eyes

Wide

Open

3

EYES WIDE OPEN

Man, I thought I was so tough all those years of being able to not show emotion no matter how bad I was hurting inside. I really felt like a true badass when on the day's things were the hardest and I was faced with some of the most painful, uncomfortable emotions I could put a game face on and just kick-butt anyway. I mean, I really thought *what good would it ever do for me to sit and explore how shitty I felt.* My role models for strength and courage never sat and talked about their feelings. Even if I had been willing to really acknowledge how I felt, I wouldn't know what to do with it anyway.

I was in such a weird place. I felt like everything I worked for, all the relationships I made, places that I had found my value in, even the things that I felt defined me were gone in a matter of weeks. For some reason, I had envisioned I would sell the company for this crazy low price and it would still allow me to have my friends and community while I explored my next chapter. But no. It was all gone. The mental picture I have is me standing in a vast open land. Behind me looks leveled like rubble as far back as the eye can see. But when I looked ahead, I was staring out into the unknown. Places I'd never been to.

When I say all my shit came up. I mean all my shit came up. Although, I had firmly resolved that I would not move forward without doing it differently this time, I didn't know exactly what that meant. For example, I didn't sit down and go *OK it's time to feel my feelings*. Haha. But it was almost as if the decision to create a different life that didn't continue to perpetuate the pain of my past was enough to crack open the door for something new to enter. I'd been too busy building, working, surviving, worrying about what everyone thought of me, and putting out fires to have even allowed a new door to open.

There was a small part of me that felt exhilarated by the possibility of something new but the fear and feelings of shame and rejection -ultimately pain- shoved those feelings of excitement far into the corner of my experience. I chose to stop running for the first time. I would find out what exactly I had been running from. When the student is ready, the teachers really do appear.

I had always considered myself a primarily internally referenced person, which to many seemed like pure stubbornness. This would prove to ultimately be one of my greatest strengths . It allowed me to question everything without needing outside approval. It was time for new information. I understood that what I knew about myself and life had brought me to the point where I was and by pure logic, I understood it was time for me to learn something new to get to a different place. My internal readiness sent out a new message that seemed to come from my soul-- a new frequency spanning into the universe. God answered my call. I was led to book after book, which led me to the practices and new understandings that began to wake me up. Which I will go into throughout later chapters in more detail. But for now, let's just say for the first time I could actually be aware of what I was thinking and notice how I was feeling. This was not in a--talk therapy, analytical, let's work through the problems of your past--kind of way. It began with my present life in real-time.

I dove in headfirst for about a year. As much as that perfect shit storm had leveled my life, it created a massive opportunity for an entirely new one to emerge. But, again, at the time, I wasn't focused on the opportunity, I was focused on gaining a completely new understanding. I had to experience life differently than I had been living. I plunged deep into neuroscience, epigenetics, case studies, meditation, prayer, mindfulness, heart coherence, frequency, neurolinguistic programming, yoga, holistic and integrative health care approaches, and gained a much better experience with God in the universe. Paradigms and worldviews that I had held and never questioned crumbled to the ground. The cornerstones of what I believed my identity to be were replaced with new things that I had never considered. It was almost as if that year and the years leading up to it were my chrysalis years. By the end of that year, I emerged from the chrysalis for the first time. My wings were wet and I was barely able to fly but I was ready to be here. Ready to live this life. I had become my own version of a butterfly. Albeit, cheesy but I love butterflies.

There was an emotional roller coaster. Truth be told, I realized I had always been on an emotional roller coaster but had been white-knuckling it with my eyes shut tight. Now I was going to have a different experience. So if I was starting to deal with things in real-time and I wasn't running anymore. What did that look like? Well, it looked like me feeling extremely uncomfortable 99% of the time. Basically, when I was sleeping, I was comfortable and little moments here and there I was comfortable. What I had been running from was beginning to make more and more sense by the day.

I became aware of my thought life. Sounds simple enough. I began to learn things like humans have around 60-70 thousand thoughts per day, but we are aware of maybe 5% of them. Apparently, 90% of those 60-70 thousand thoughts per day are the same as the day before. It turns out that our thoughts inform a ton of our feelings which then drive our behaviors which then add up to our life. So phase 1 for me was to begin to notice what the heck I was thinking about. I have to say that I really felt like I knew what I thought about when I embarked on this. I discovered I had no idea. I was shocked.

I didn't do anything fancy. I just decided *OK I'm gonna start to pay attention to what I think about*. I did not expect to be surprised. I didn't even take this practice too seriously until I had read several books on neuroscience, quantum physics, and watched a few documentaries. I was very interested in gaining a new understanding of how we really work and how I can really change. For some reason. noticing and thinking about what I was thinking about just didn't seem like that big of a deal until I really understood how and why it worked. So I committed to noticing. And here are some of the most common reoccurring thoughts that I was having:

- *You don't know what you're doing.*
- *I'm not smart enough.*
- *I hate myself.*
- *I'm a terrible mom, Kai deserves better.*
- *Nothing I do ever works out.*
- *I'm not good enough and never have been and I never will be.*
- *I don't deserve to be happy.*
- *I'm a bad person.*
- *I am worthless.*
- *Everyone hates me.*
- *Somethings terribly wrong with me no wonder no one wants to be my friend.*
- *My life is ruined.*
- *I screw everything up.*
- *I'm afraid I'll never be OK.*
- *I'm a failure.*
- *I'm terrified.*
- *I am ashamed to be who I am.*

These are just a few and they don't include the thoughts that were more in story form that I'd play and replay in my mind about past painful problems or future painful potentials. Mainly my thoughts were focused on what went wrong and what else could go wrong and in general what was wrong with me. Here's something to note, when I read that list, I thought *how am I not a depressing Eeyore to be around?* I mean that sounds like a total Debbie Downer. But I wasn't. I said optimistic things. I generally expressed a positive attitude. I've always loved humor. I laughed and made jokes constantly.

The feedback I would get from people was often how happy and confident I was. It was eye-opening to see how much I was able to hide my feelings, even from myself. Being very psychoanalytical, I had naturally already psychoanalyzed my life. I could list out stories and circumstances of things that had happened throughout my life, confident those were the things that had caused my unhappiness. I saw myself as an overcomer and resilient but deep down, I really felt broken.

When I began to pay attention to what I was thinking specifically-I was taken back. I remember feeling this push and pull at first, wanting to know more to get into an empowered place in my life. But, honestly, paying attention to all the thoughts that were running through my mind was really rough at first and really painful. I could see what I had been trying to run from. They were just going on every day all day in the backdrop of whatever I was doing or saying. At first, I would just notice a thought here and there and I would think *wow that was harsh*. But as I became more and more open to really seeing what I was thinking, I developed an ability that I didn't even know I had.

Turns out that all humans have this ability called metacognition. It reminds me of when I inadvertently learned to understand and speak Spanish. In High School, I took Spanish for several years and got A's and B's in it but interestingly, I had no ability to speak Spanish. I guess

I wasn't learning with the intention of retaining and applying the knowledge. Years later, I became the lead physiotherapist for a medical group in town. I would see their patients throughout the day. About 30% of the patient population was primarily Spanish-speaking. I had a full-time medical assistant assigned to me as my translator with those patients. I wished I knew Spanish, but I didn't.

I remember when I first started, all the words sounded so fast and foreign and it just felt like I would never be able to understand or speak it. And I didn't have to because I had a translator. However, after about six months, I remember I started thinking *I feel like everyone's talking slower because I can hear the breaks between the words.* I would find myself knowing what was being said without trying. As time went on, I knew how to respond in Spanish. I suppose it would be considered immersion. I'll never forget the stark contrast between when I first started, so many fast sounds strung together without stopping and in the end, I could understand and speak the language.

Becoming aware of what I was thinking about felt like that. At first, it just seemed overwhelming and kind of ineffectual. Then, I began to notice fast and sudden thoughts here and there. Until one day, I could just clearly hear all the thoughts that were running through my mind and somehow, I was separate from them. There was some part of me that was able to just notice all of the thoughts one after the other as they ran through my mind.

I remember a turning point and I noted it in my book *I*

AM Happy. Healthy. Free. and now with more back story, it may shed new light on it.

I was putting my son's clothes away in his room one afternoon. There was nothing notable happening that day. It was just a day in my life. As I was walking across his room, I became aware of a voice. It was talking incessantly about what I needed to get done, what I hadn't done right, and it was talking so harshly to me, it was demanding so much of me and reminded me of every negative thing it could. It was just a constant stream of stressful words I noticed my heartbeat was fast, my body was tense, my breathing was shallow. I started putting Kai's clothes away more quickly. I felt like such a failure. *I can't do anything right. I need to do better, I need to hurry...* and then I stopped dead in my tracks. I physically stopped moving. It hit me... It felt like time just slowed down.

I looked at Kai's clothes in my hands, I looked around the room. *It's just me in this room putting my little boys' clothes away and I'm screaming at myself on the inside.* In that moment, I became aware that no one had ever treated me as badly as I had treated myself. I saw it. In my mind, I saw me waking up in the morning instantly berating myself until I finally fell asleep at night. Thinking, thinking, thinking, replaying, reminding, warning, demanding, humiliating, this was the way I communicated with myself. My eyes filled with tears and I saw myself as a little girl standing there with messy curly brown hair wide-eyed. I saw *me*. She was precious. *I am so sorry. I love you and I'm not going to treat you like this anymore.* No one had ever treated me worse than I was treating me.

At that moment, I became my number one fan. The voice that had abused my life lost its power. I may have wanted to make a change for years, but life exists in moments. I experienced my light. Our ability to become aware of our thoughts is a gateway to newfound freedom. Often, we just run on autopilot with a thought free-for-all going on. Remember we have 60 to 70,000 measured thoughts each day and 95% of those are the same as the day before. And with our thoughts come feelings.

Cultivating the skill of awareness specifically in my thought life put me in the driver's seat but harnessing the power of my emotions is what gave me the gas to get where I wanted to go. Freedom. I didn't have to run anymore, and the rest of the book will unfold why you don't either and teach you how to harness the power of your own emotions.

Every human has thoughts and emotions. No matter what, that part is not optional but *not every human learns how to navigate their thoughts and emotions to create a completely different life experience.* It's our choice just like everything else. So I stopped running. I noticed that my thinking was and had been hammering away at me for years. Noticing the content of my thoughts was a surprise, I was shocked at what level I absolutely did not want to feel all the things that I was feeling --without pouring myself into overachievement or self-destructing to avoid the pain. But I sat in it and here's how.

Feel
Your
Feelings

Stop! Take the next 5 minutes to get
acquainted with your thoughts. You don't have
to be in a quiet place or secluded. You just
have to listen. What are you saying to yourself?
Write your thoughts down here.

_____

_____

_____

_____

_____

_____

_____

_____

_____

_____

1

Angry Kitty

4

ANGRY KITTY

If you can't handle the heat, then you need to get out of the kitchen. I don't even know where that saying came from, but it rings true when I think of how I felt trying to learn how not to run from how I feel. I used to think that going back and somehow healing what's happened in the past would heal the present. There is some merit to that in terms of gaining new understanding and maybe changing the way you felt about something, so you'd stop feeling that terrible way in the present—which makes sense. But really it was never about what actually happened then or now when it all shook out, it was being able to *handle how I feel about whatever happened then or now.*

I can look back on that day in second-grade and my entire class, my peers vocally and heatedly expressed that they did not want me on their team – *how I felt about what happened and how I wasn't able to handle how I felt about what happened really became the issue that lasted.* So I can go back and possibly recreate what happened in my mind and tell myself a different story but, ultimately, I'm back to feeling feelings. This is where I'd get stuck. Trying to change or handle how I felt. I felt ashamed, sad, humiliated and afraid. I hated how terrible those feelings felt and I did everything I could to keep them at bay understandably.

Throughout my life growing up and as a young adult, I continued to amass more and more of these feelings and I just became more and more averse to feeling them. I realized after my life exploded that so much had built up inside that it just felt like I couldn't run anymore. I didn't want to. Trying to deal with emotions through the analytical mind can only take us so far. At the end of the day, you feel how you feel whether we admit it or not. The thing about emotions, they don't go away until they're acknowledged or expressed. As badly as we want ignoring them to work, ignoring them just lets them fester longer in the body. There are more books on this topic in science, psychology, and spirituality. I won't go into all of the ins and outs of emotions getting stuck in the body but trust me when I say they do. Before we go into how to deal with expressing emotion, we first need to talk about how to first get yourself willing to feel what you're feeling or acknowledge what you're feeling in the first place.

———

Here was my experience. Much like making the decision to become aware of what I was thinking, I made the decision to become aware of how I was actually feeling. There were many experiences, I'm tempted to say countless, throughout the year where I wanted to bolt but didn't. I can remember one particular time that highlighted just how much this was a struggle for me. I had begun the practice of meditating. No particular dogma or rigid guidelines- just a practice of me setting time aside to sit down and focus on my breath and just be there. No distractions, no getting stuck in future pondering, or the past, just being there in the present moment with each breath.

I had come from the health and fitness arena and, as you already know, I was used to going 100 miles an hour. I would have much preferred doing hard-core workouts, hitting punching bags, lifting weights, cardio, anything besides silence and stillness. Sitting and focusing on my breath felt like watching paint dry while having massive anxiety at the same time. But again I had researched so much at this point and meditation proved to be one of the most effective ways for me to change my inner world which I had also come to understand directly affects my outer world. So, I committed to meditation. I continued to find myself sitting on my couch enduring many meditations where I sat uncomfortably noticing every itch on my nose, dog barking, mind racing, etc. until my timer went off and I could check meditation off my list for the day.

One torture-session/meditation was different. I sat there, closed my eyes and began taking long slow deep breaths. I had learned that it was not about me pushing thoughts away or *trying* to meditate, just allow whatever comes up to come up and just be there with it. Whatever it was. I could feel the knots in my sacral area just under my rib cage and I noticed that my heart almost felt like it was burning kind of like heartburn. I felt so anxious inside, but

I just kept breathing and I just kept having the thought *allow it* to make space for whatever *it* was. As I continued breathing, the burning in my heart increased and the knots in my stomach seemed to get tighter and expand at the same time. Needless to say, I was extremely uncomfortable. I even had the thought cross my mind *maybe I'm getting sick?* But then a thought or whatever you want to call it came to me- *it's OK to feel the pain* and, for a second, it's like I had to catch my breath. The thought continued *you don't need to control it or understand it or interact with it. Just allow it to do whatever it needs to do and when it's ready it will go. You can't force it or judge it.* It's almost as if I intuitively knew this was regarding the pain that I was holding onto inside:

I felt sadness. I felt shame. I felt fear. Anger. All of it was reverberating throughout my body. I thought *I don't have to run, and I am strong enough to feel all of these feelings. I don't need to make them stop. I am making room for them.* My body was tense from head to toe, my heart felt like it was on fire, my stomach even felt like it was burning but I just sat there taking deep slow breaths with my eyes closed allowing myself to feel whatever came up. I knew that somehow, I could trust this process. I'm not sure of the time that actually passed but at some point, all of the intensity and extreme discomfort just started to die down on its own.

I wasn't rushing it. I wasn't trying to make it stop or go away. I just allowed it to be there and do what it needed to do. Even though the feelings were so strong my body was physically responding to them, I didn't run. I had such a profound realization. At the time, I didn't really understand on what level it was going to change my life, but I did know then it was a big deal. I realized *it's OK to be incredibly uncomfortable.* I don't need to *make* myself feel better. Even the hardest of emotions just need to be acknowledged and they will go when they're ready and that's OK.

I was able to see my pattern so clearly now--every time I had an uncomfortable emotion, I just wanted it to go away or stop. I would immediately delve into psychoanalyzing and explaining away what I was feeling, or I would just completely suppress it by getting busy. Running like this had some pretty serious side effects, I hadn't realized my massive fear of hard feelings had kept me in a constant state of damage control. I could never just relax. My fear of feeling bad, ironically made me feel worse.

Being so focused on trying to control outcomes and keeping these terrible feelings at bay really was a full-time job. I could never really let myself feel all the good emotions either because you can't suppress one side without suppressing the other. I was so concerned about the other shoe dropping. If I was feeling happy, I'd begin to think *what if it goes away.* I just couldn't get comfortable in the present time.

I went to this private conference/retreat recommended by one of my friends who is a doctor and it was someone she highly admired. So I went by myself for five days. The conference host talked about *loving what is.* I liked this idea of "loving what is" then but it has continued to reveal itself to me in much greater depth over the years. Today, I am 100% OK with feeling like shit. It passes and there's no rush. It's part of happiness and health. That used to be so counterintuitive for me. I thought if I was experiencing rough feelings that it meant something bad. I am able to feel happiness, joy, peace, patience, etc. without being worried that it's somehow going to go away and not come back. I'm not worried that I'm going to feel things like sadness, anger, frustration, pain, guilt, or shame. Of course I am, sometimes. I have embraced being human.

Today, I am OK with all of those feelings. They're just feelings, they cannot be ignored and they're not the end of the world. In fact, they usually help by giving good insight. Maybe I need to slow down. Maybe something needs to be adjusted in a relationship or a friendship. Maybe there's something that I should be doing that would help me or bring me closer to my goals. I welcome the full spectrum of human emotion because they all serve a purpose. I don't live in any one emotion all of the time. Here's the funny thing, I've never been more OK with feeling any of the human emotions and, ironically, I feel better than I ever have before. So it would seem the answer to bringing more peace and empowerment into our lives is to allow and acknowledge how we feel. Here are a few of the things I ran into that are important to note.

Once I began acknowledging how I felt or acknowledging feelings as they would come up in the present time, I would find myself wanting to really dig into them. I would want to find the cause of what made me feel that way. I really wanted to get judgmental or blame-y about my feelings. There's nothing wrong necessarily about having a desire to understand what triggered certain emotions. However, this can rapidly turn into a time-sucking vortex that can come with a whole new set of problems. For example, when I realized how worthless I felt inside, I wanted to know why I felt worthless. So I would go on these long, drawn-out, deep-dives into my past trying to discover why I felt worthless. I would find lots of stories and circumstances that definitely had prompted feelings of worthlessness. But then what?

There's just a point that I personally hit where it really doesn't matter so much to me to attempt to find the root cause of every emotion that I have. If it's important for me to know what prompted the emotion. I'm always open to it and it will generally come to me and help me out in some way but, for the very most part, I just allow the rough emotions to come up just like I do the good ones. I mean that I don't need to know exactly why I feel happy every time I feel happy. So I really don't need to know why I feel sad every time I feel sad.

Further, there tended to be a strong desire in me back then to want to blame someone or something for how I felt. Again, this can become a real stuck point because what if someone hurt you? You feel sad and betrayed - you can't go back and make the person un-hurt you and you can't not feel how you feel. Really the only thing that is a sure-fire way to keep you healthy and moving forward is to say, *yeah, I'm hurt. I feel sad and betrayed and I don't need to make myself feel a different way. I'm just going to allow these feelings to be here and know that they will go when they are ready. I won't ignore them, force them to go or obsess over causation.*

This can be very difficult if you desire justice. If you

need someone to pay for making you feel bad. This again can become not only another time-sucking vortex but a life-sucking one as well. If you play that scenario all the way out let's say someone hurts you. You feel hurt and betrayed. You desire justice and you find a way for them to be paid back or to punish them in some way-- Did all of that energy and activity take away your pain? Did it actually affect the only thing that is truly able to harm you? No. The pain, the betrayal, the sadness, if it was never acknowledged and you jumped straight to justice and blame. Then those emotions will stay with you until you are able to sit with them. There are a couple of things that have no place in a life filled with freedom, expansion, and forward momentum. These things are blame and judgment.

It is very difficult to allow yourself to acknowledge painful emotions as they come when there is a strong need to assign blame or judgment to the cause of the emotion. It is an illusion that the ball ever actually leaves your court. If your focus is truly to learn how to optimally navigate your human experience then it is important to understand the purpose of acknowledging and allowing space for your feelings.

Some people have carried the emotion of anger their entire life. For example, I know that I did for most of mine but interestingly, the actual emotion of anger is only active in the body for a matter of minutes. After that period of time, the continued experience of anger is brought on by the person continuing to remember, revive, and relive it. After but a matter of moments, the anger is on life-support - if you want to continue the anger-think more thoughts to keep the flame burning or by simply not acknowledging it at all- you'll stay pissed for a loooong time. Possibly your lifetime. In my case, it was in more of a Lego Kitty Unicorn way-- overly nice until one day you explode.

Another fun thing about suppressing emotion is that we generally want to make sense of everything. With this desire, we quickly categorize and assign meaning, definition, cause, category, etc. We put everything we feel as quickly as we can into a box that we already understand. This is important for being able to function on a daily basis. Imagine if we had to re-understand or think in-depth about everything we saw, heard, felt, etc. in a day. We would be a wreck. However, it's important to be mindful of this desire to quickly make sense of things when it comes to our internal world especially our emotions.

I grew up feeling and holding onto a lot of rejection and shame-- I filtered life through that lens. I held beliefs like *people will hurt me and leave me because something is wrong with me*. I was terrified of rejection. As I went through life, I subconsciously scanned for rejection. I was constantly mitigating and analyzing every situation and relationship for potential rejection. Interestingly, I found myself being rejected often. Some were catastrophic rejections like my perfect shit storm. Some were heartbreaking rejections by the majority of my serious relationships. Others were more subtle and flew under the radar. Either way it's almost like I become a magnet for rejection.

You don't have to be a scientific genius or spiritual guru to recognize that whatever we're heavily focused on really ends up showing up in our life. We seem to readily accept this on more positive notes. For example, Angela wanted to go to the Olympics so she focused on it, thought about it, obsessed over it, and had consistent behavior over a long period of time that resulted in Angela going to the Olympics. See. We're not shocked, it makes perfect sense. But when it comes to undesired outcomes we don't understand. Let's use me as an example. Erica was terrified she would be rejected by the people that she cared about so she thought about it and focused on how afraid she was of that happening. She kept her eye on her worst fear for a consistent and long period of time. Erica was rejected a lot.

You get what you focus on. There's no blame in that. There's also no judgment. It just is. Being judgmental or wielding blame will just make it impossible to be with your emotions. Have you ever been around a person that makes a bad situation worse with their judgment? If you've ever run out of gas, you're the one sitting on the side of the road, you're the one that's already in a really bad spot with it and yet the person that comes to help you can only talk about how stupid it was that you forgot to put gas in your car. Yes, that's an example from my life. Don't be that person to yourself it'll make the process feel like hell-- remember that critic I had to get rid of inside of me. She had good intentions with all her safety concerns and self-protection strategies but honestly, she's the one that almost broke me for real. We've got to be able to feel our emotions without judging ourselves half to death or blaming someone.

Living a life with the inability to be honest with

ourselves about how we feel creates a stunted life. It doesn't matter how big your life looks, only you know if you feel small and contracted inside. A significant aspect of feeling small and contracted is not tapping into the unlimited strength we have when we embrace the power of our emotions. If you want to live a big life, you have to make enough room for you to expand. Make enough room for *all of yourself*. I have room in my life today for angry Kitty, happy Kitty, sad Kitty, scared Kitty, peaceful Kitty...all my Kitty's.

Feel
Your
Feelings

Let's be honest!
What feelings do you hate feeling?
List the feelings that always
knock you off balance.
What circumstances bring them up?

_____

_____

_____

_____

_____

_____

_____

_____

_____

_____

_____

_____

_____

5

When Dreams Don't Come True

WHEN DREAMS DON'T COME TRUE

M y mantra for years has been Never Give Up, a quote by Winston Churchill. I found such strength in it. It was like my one solid guidepost no matter what circumstances or challenges I was facing. I just knew if I didn't give up, I would make it. These words were the one thing I could cling to before I knew how to navigate my inner world. They still ring very true today. I believe it with all of my heart that not giving up is a cornerstone in getting to our desired destinations.

That being said, everything I did prior to understanding my internal world always felt like such a struggle. I worked so hard for every inch I gained. Everything I built, every relationship I had. It was as if nothing came without the proverbial blood, sweat, and tears. But knowing what I know now, I look back and in contrast to my life experience today, progress and achievement just might not need to be as brutal as I've experienced them in the past. It's almost as if I had a firmly held belief that you have to sacrifice everything or you really didn't earn it. Therefore, you don't deserve it. Ew!

It occurred to me somewhere along my journey, post-perfect shit storm, that I was fighting to earn my place in this world. I struggled with feeling like an imposter. Believing I really didn't deserve to be here but if I could just work hard enough and add enough value, my existence would be acceptable. We'll dive into feeling like enough and the plague of feeling like an imposter in chapter 7 but for now, I just wanted to make a point that I didn't know what was happening inside of me. I just clung to never giving up and I got pretty far with that.

I achieved some very special milestones scholastically, professionally, in business, and financially. The wins always felt great but I seemed to be that person that if there were 100 yes's and 1 no, I would focus on the no. Or if there were five successes and five failures, I could only think about the failures. This proves to be a real problem if you're trying to avoid feeling bad. If I hit a milestone, I would immediately start working towards the next thing and analyze what I could've done better. I couldn't let myself celebrate wins. I didn't know how to be comfortable feeling good or bad. Happiness felt fleeting and sadness was always on my heels. I've always loved setting goals and working towards them which is great but somewhere along the way it had gotten distorted for me. It's as if the goals defined me and my value. I suppose it explains why I was so crazy about making sure that I achieved when I had set out to do each task, in my mind, my worth hung in the balance. God help me when I would fail to hit my target.

I used to oscillate between two general categories of goal-setters. Some that don't even set the goal because they don't want to risk failing--they can't handle the feelings that would come with that. And some that will set the goal and risk everything to achieve it because they couldn't handle the feelings of failure. Either way trying to cope with dreams not coming true can really dictate the quality of life. I mean it really begs the question of what hurts worse; to know that none of your dreams are going to come true because deep down you know you're not even really going after them or going after them with everything you've got and it not working out the way you planned? I've had a lot of the second one and a little of the first one.

When I started to become really comfortable not avoiding pain, I was able to see more clearly where I would get stuck the most. Through talking with many others, I saw that the experience of failure really set people back- including myself- at times. I've always been very resilient, resourceful, and optimistic about what's possible despite the landslide of heavy emotions I had going on inside of me. I truly believe I can thank both of my parents for those wonderful characteristics. They have embodied those traits my whole life and I have seen them show up in the face of adversity as a couple of champions.

Looking back, I saw that as I would be moving towards achieving a goal, many of my insecurities, worries, and fears would be rumbling under the surface and I would work harder and harder and harder to make sure I didn't fail. When I would succeed I'd be able to continue to move forward quickly onto the next thing. All of the emotions that I would keep at bay would put me through the wringer and I would feel exhausted and overwhelmed but by God, I hit my goals.

Now picture the same thing- all of the emotions, insecurities, hopes, excitement and then the goal falling apart. Sometimes it would be because I made a mistake. Sometimes it would be because someone else made a mistake but either way, sometimes I'd be sitting with failure. The feelings surrounding those experiences I noted were by far some of the most difficult to push away and as it turns out some of the most difficult to sit with and feel. My perfect shit storm experience hands-down felt like my ultimate failure, it was like the Holy Grail of my worst nightmare. My career, my relationships, and my finances-- were all devastated at the exact same time wrapped in a gigantic bow of rejection. It's moments like these when the rubber meets the road. When a theory is forced into practice and you find out what actually works versus what is an ungrounded, BS, word of advice on how to get through life. As someone who has definitely experienced loss and failure before and prior to that moment, whether it's big or small, I can attest; failure can make you want to shrink back.

As we know I chose to expand but getting back on the famous horse was terrifying. I just wanted to hide in the safety of my home with my son and husband. I had a few close friends that I am not sure how I would've gotten through that time without. Past that, I did not want to be seen. I did not want to be hurt again like that and I didn't want to fail. I started merging into that category where maybe if I just didn't set goals then I wouldn't need to achieve them and I could bypass all the vulnerability completely. It turns out, at least in my experience, that *the pain of stagnation or shrinking is worse than the pain of giving it your all and losing*. I tried to be small for almost 2 years. Those two years were remarkable for my internal learning and growth which laid the foundation for me to show up and navigate life better than I have ever imagined. But I knew then I would need to risk failure again and, for the first time, I was strong enough to really acknowledge it but I was fucking terrified.

I had to put all of my newfound internal skills into practice and really truly move forward. It was two steps forward one step back. It kind of reminded me of my shark phobia. Yes, I have a shark phobia. I watched Jaws obsessively when I was young and I'm originally from Colorado so I lived nowhere near the ocean. At 12 years old, my dad took my sister and me to California for the first time to see the ocean and I discovered that I had a phobia of sharks. I'll never forget --he rented a light blue convertible-- the true California dreaming experience. I saw palm trees for the first time as we drove up and parked right in front of the beach in Venice. I had talked obsessively for months about my excitement to see the ocean for the first time. I was filled with excitement, sharks had never even crossed my mind.

When the car parked, I excitedly unbuckled and cleared the side of the convertible without even opening the door so I could run towards the ocean, tearing off my shoes while still in motion. As I got about 1 foot away from reaching the water it was as if I hit an invisible wall that stopped me frozen in my tracks. I broke into a panic, sweating from head to toe, I could hardly breathe and I was suddenly gripped with fear. As my dad and sister caught up to me and realized that something was frightfully wrong, I was gasping, *I can't go in. I can't go in.* My dad was frantically looking around for what on earth had happened. He thought I had cut myself or hurt myself. He finally said, *"Erica what is wrong!"* The words flew out of my mouth *"Dad! There are sharks in there! I can't go in!"*

I had no idea that fear was in me?! I couldn't even believe what was coming out of my mouth. Weirdly from there, it turned into me not being able to swim in lakes if I couldn't see through the water around me. I couldn't close my eyes in a swimming pool and even occasionally would panic when my eyes were closed in the bathtub or the shower. To those of you that have experienced a phobia, you know exactly what I'm talking about. To those of you who haven't, well you might understand it more than you know when you hear the parallel between this and my journey forward from feelings of failure.

As I continued to venture forward into the unknown spanning out in front of me, I was determined to create something new. Something that didn't look and feel like my past and I understood now that would require me to think, feel, and act differently than I had before. By societal standards I had been quite successful; a great education, successful business owner, built a seven-figure company from scratch, a happy healthy son and I had also married the love of my life. Yet I knew the internal climate of what my life had been and I was plagued with the feeling that at the peak of my success to date- I was still so stressed.

I knew moving forward I wanted to create more wonderful things that helped people. Only this time, I was going to do it without running scared. When I first started getting opportunities to speak, I would feel panic sweeping over me not for fear of public speaking but for fear of getting back on the horse and being seen. I had a vision and a desire to help people learn what I was learning and decided to write my first book. This prompted every feeling of insecurity, fear, and overwhelm in me. Each time I would sit down to write it felt like I was running up to the ocean's edge and discovering a phobia. My thoughts would run wild with

- *This could be my ultimate failure.*
- *I'm going to be rejected more than I ever have.*
- *You're a loser how are you going to write a book?*
- *No one cares.*
- *You don't have what it takes, you're going to fail.*

and with those thoughts I would have these feelings:

- Paralyzing fear
- Anxiety
- Shame
- Sadness
- A strong sense of unworthiness
- Bouts of panic

I would acknowledge those thoughts and sit down and let those feelings wash over me without fighting them, without running. I would just take long deep breaths telling my emotions that it's OK to feel what I'm feeling. They can do what they need to do and go when they're ready.

The new thoughts that I would think, as I would observe the steady stream of thoughts filled with fear:

- *It's worth it to me to show up.*
- *It's OK to be afraid.*
- *You are enough.*
- *I love you.*
- *Keep moving forward.*

This went on for months and I rebuilt brick by brick. I would think *my racing mind desires to protect me from hurt. I'm safe and I'm moving forward.*

Once I really understood that my feelings were powerful but that I was the one in charge, I found total peace. Feeling bad wasn't going to take me out. I began to feel unstoppable. It started with facing my greatest fear and surviving but what took me to the next level was being able to feel fear or any emotion and only get stronger not by avoiding it but by integrating it to serve me at a higher level. By logic, I've always said that failure is a critical aspect of success because if we're not willing to fail then that means we're not willing to try anything new which doesn't create many paths to succeed in.

In my opinion, dreams don't actually die. They just continue to reshape themselves to reflect the desires of our hearts as we evolve. When a forest burns down the ash provides some of the richest nutrients on earth for regrowth. Willingness to feel our emotions creates the ability to move forward from an empowered place. If I wouldn't have been willing to learn to notice what was running through my mind and then learn to allow myself to feel my emotions--I can guarantee you that I might have built another success story on paper but it wouldn't be this one and I would probably be on the brink of collapse internally-- missing my life because I was too scared to feel it.

Feel
Your
Feelings

Do you have a dream that "died"?
How do you feel about that? Is it truly gone
forever? Or has it reshaped itself?
Explore here!

_____

_____

_____

_____

_____

_____

_____

_____

_____

_____

_____

The
Fundamentals

6

THE FUNDAMENTALS

Once you open a new door to seeking a new understanding, you will be guided to information or practices that will serve you best on your journey as you move forward. There are so many wonderful modalities, practices, and so much research to assist us. However, there are some key fundamentals that can serve nearly everyone. They don't cost money and they are very powerful. I've done my best to talk about a few of the ones that help me the most and that I know could be transformative for you as well.

I don't know about you but when I initially thought about really wanting to gain a new handle on navigating my inner world, I immediately associated it with lots of time and talking and possibly rehashing of my past with therapist. Which I believe can be extremely useful and in fact, I've benefited greatly from that practice in my later teenage years. I met with a counselor two to three times a week for months and then dropped to once a week until I left for college. So my first instinct was that I should get a therapist. That didn't end up being what I was led to. I had a hard time with some of the practices that I was finding not because they were too hard but because they were seemingly not hard enough.

Remember, I tended to think that if it wasn't a struggle or really difficult then somehow it's less valuable. I discovered the most powerful tools to help me were free and available to me anytime, anywhere and in complete abundance. I did a lot of research on my end to really ensure the validity of these practices. Truthfully, free and easily accessible practices didn't sound serious enough to touch what I had going on with a ten-foot pole. This really exposed my belief system. In America, we tend to undervalue things that are free or easily accessible. If it doesn't cost money, if it didn't come from a doctor, or you didn't work really, really, really, hard for it then it's probably worthless, right?! Wrong. There are some things that are free and easy and extremely valuable. Before you blow me off when you read the next sentence-- trust me when I say this works.

BREATH.

Our breath. Breathing. Breath is something we have all been doing since we were born. We're doing it right now and we'll continue until our last breath. I had no understanding of how breathing is a fundamental tool for creating an optimal life experience beyond the obvious of oxygenating the body. I completely took it for granted. I've always felt thankful that I'm breathing but at the same time not really thinking about it.

Breath brings me into the present moment. This is monumental because I was living primarily in the past or in the future up until my perfect shitstorm year that changed my life. What do I mean by living in the past or in the future and not in the present moment? First, I would say more accurately, I was living mostly in the past, of course without consciously meaning to. You know having 60,000+ thoughts per day and the majority of those thoughts being the same as the day before. With most thoughts dominantly rooted in the past, it's safe to say, on default, we're living in yesterday. Replaying problems, stories, and events--things that have already happened filters each new moment through the past. Apparently, living mostly in the past can really promote depressive feelings.

Sometimes, I would be living in the future. For me, it was often positive, planning and thinking about something I was trying to achieve in the future. My mind would also turn to more of the worrying and stressing about the potential problems of tomorrow based on the problems of my past. My ability to just *be* wherever I was, truly be in the present moment, was very limited. I really didn't understand what I was doing at the time so it really didn't concern me. I wasn't able to truly engage with my life in real-time which is where life actually takes place. The present moment is the only place where we can truly affect change in our life. Everything else has either already happened or hasn't happened yet. The present moment is the only thing that's *actually happening*.

For example, when I would be talking to someone often my mind would be racing into worries of the future or worries of the past. I was completely unaware of this but I was rarely right there present, fully in the conversation. It wasn't hard to see why I was generally anywhere but here in light of discovering how truly uncomfortable I was with navigating my internal world. Very specifically allowing myself to feel whatever I was feeling in the moment without a judgmental reaction was quite foreign.

It's quite common for humans to live in future worries or the excitement of tomorrow or the past memories of regret or happiness-- remaining present in one's own life is trained out of us early on. I think our natural state is to be present with what is. When I say trained out of that state of presence, I don't think it's because big humans want little humans to learn something that would harm them. In fact, I think it's quite the opposite. We try to teach each other what we know and often with the intention of helping or preparation. Parents teaching children, teachers teaching children, well no one taught them about the importance and the power of living in the present moment. We can't teach what we ourselves don't know.

It's just by default the practice of presence is not cultivated in many of our lives. Many of the things we teach each other are rooted in love but are motivated by fear. Especially with children, they are warned about everything with good intentions, trying to make sure that they will survive. As valuable as it is to teach your children to look both ways before crossing the street to avoid being hit by a car there should also be a moment where we say the same regarding their emotions. Notice how you feel. It's safe to feel, it will pass, and it might even help you gain a new understanding. If you push it down and suppress it, it will build up and really control your life. It's like we train our children to be these warriors to go out in the world and survive and yet many of them are terrified of their own emotions mostly because they're not talked about or understood. The breath offers more than just the gift of life it's also your portal to present time living which I would argue is actually living.

Breathing with intention and focus draws the mind and the emotions from wherever they're running and grounds them into the present moment. It can take the body from the state of fight, flight, or paralysis in a matter of minutes and often seconds to calmness. This is a practice that Navy SEALs use along with the most peaceful people on earth. This can be used to get in front of and create a space for any thought patterns and emotions that are flooding in and turn the moment into a completely different experience.

If anger wells up, take slow intentional deep breaths and watch what happens. If your mind is racing and you feel really anxious, take slow deep breaths. Remember it's not about making the emotions stop. It's creating the space for them to be acknowledged, expressed, and in turn sets you free. Intentional breathing gives you this powerful tool to move out of reaction and into response.

Response allows you to access the information that will best serve the moment versus an automatic, pre-canned reaction to patterns of the past and emotional triggers coming from a time and place that no longer exists. You can interact with your real-life from a new place. The breath, slow and intentional, also refills your energy in your mind, body, and spirit, as it is filled with information and critical elements that will regenerate you. When you're feeling drained, blocked, or overwhelmed, begin taking slow, deep, intentional inhales and exhales, focusing on your breath and watch what happens to your creativity.

There are lots of reasons why practicing breath and presence isn't readily acknowledged with the merit it deserves in assisting the human experience in the American culture. I go into greater depth on this in *I Am Happy. Healthy. Free.* but in short, it's really rooted in how our culture perceives matters of the mind and spirit. They are basically considered unknowable therefore most of our approaches to health and wellness address only the physical body using protocols such as medication and matters of the mind and spirit are considered secondary issues that can be approached through hundreds of different frameworks all of which land in the "optional" categories.

Although we've talked about living in the present moment and breath-work assisting in doing so, we have to want to live in the present moment. I know that when I first learned the value of living in the present moment I struggled with it. Curiously, I imagined that living in the here and now, actually setting the intention to live in the here and now, would mean that I would slow down, become less productive and frankly it sounded irresponsible. In my mind, I viewed all of my worrying, planning, and future pacing as being hyper responsible and vigilant in steering my life and my family's life to safety and well-being.

I viewed my obsession with understanding my past similarly. I believed that if I could understand my past clearly then that would empower me to make sure that I didn't repeat the same mistakes in my future. Doesn't all of that sound logical and reasonable? I think so. I was worried that really trying to be present in the moment was going to make me lackadaisical and my life might spin out of control. Basically, I saw high-achievement and present moment living as mutually exclusive. I pictured monks and super chill stoners just being "super in the moment" -- not worrying about a thing. And that was never going to be me. Again, I needed more information.

Turns out living in the present moment increased my focus, productivity, creativity, critical thinking, satisfaction, energy, and overall my quality of life. Today, when I'm working on a task inside of a project I am able to get more done in less time with greater clarity and without the stress. When I'm having a conversation with someone, I actually feel like I'm connecting with them and I don't feel rushed like I need to be doing something else or the sense that I'm letting balls drop. I'm fully engaged in listening and responding. I have never felt more connected with my son and my husband and I have simultaneously never had more on my plate. The proof is in the pudding.

I didn't realize that my mind racing forward and backward diminished my potential drastically for productivity and connectivity. When I notice that I am racing forward or backward outside of the moment, I say inwardly *be here now* and slow down and deepen my breath. Occasionally, when I have shared the practice of breath and presence I've been met with concern. "Erica, that's a lot of things to think about. I am already so crazy I don't want to have to worry about something else. You don't understand what kind of stress and pressure I'm under." They clearly missed all of the points entirely but I don't blame them because, for years, I did too.

MEDITATION.

The definition: think deeply or focus one's mind for a period of time, in silence or with the aid of chanting, for religious or spiritual purposes or as a method of relaxation.

There is no one way or right way to meditate. In fact, I don't care what you call it.

- Set aside 5+ minutes.
- Stop moving (get in a comfortable position- lay down, sit down, kneel) whatever feels right to you.
- Breath deeply.
- And be there.

Meditating is not religious or spiritual unless you are. And whoever and however you feel connected to your spirituality is up to you. That being said - meditation is not a time to set aside and incessantly talk, request, run your mind etc. It's not a time where you are trying to control an outcome. It's a time where you sit, breathe, be there, and you hold the space for whatever needs to come up - you allow it, keep breathing and staying present.

You might realize something , you might feel wildly uncomfortable, you might feel nothing but racing thoughts, nervous body or a tiny bit calmer. Here's what's for sure- it will be what it needs to be for you and the practice is like plugging yourself into the wall to recharge. This puts you in a position to handle the billions/trillions of incoming and outgoing pieces of information that you are sending and receiving in every nanosecond of everyday. It's not about getting something or giving something - it's a critical and highly functional thing for humans to do so you can function optimally. It's not sexy but it's the truth.

REST.

Intentional and judgment-free rest. Sometimes emotional and mental activity can take up more energy than physical activity. There are days when I am solely sitting working on the computer exerting barely a shred of physical exertion, yet I'll feel like I have just run a marathon. These are the days where I say that I've run an emotional marathon. It's important to acknowledge and honor when we need rest. Intentional rest stems from a greater understanding of how we work best. For example, if we feel like we need a nap, sit down and close your eyes for 10 minutes and just let your mind and body relax. If we were driving our car and it started to overheat, we would have no problem pulling over on the side of the road and doing what's necessary to cool it down.

It's far too common in our culture to view rest as non-productivity or even laziness. Ironically, again, getting good sleep at night and intentionally taking downtime when you feel like you need it, actually increases productivity creativity etc. Resting without judgment is very important. It defeats the purpose if while you're setting aside time to rest and your judging yourself for needing it or wanting it. The judgment will not allow you to rest and you'll continue to drain your own energy. Instead of honoring societal standards of performance we need to be more internally referenced based on the factual messaging coming from our individual bodies. This is a far more logical and grounded approach to increasing our own ability to navigate our internal and external world.

WATER.

Water is another critical yet highly underutilized way to feeling our best. You can see the pattern here. So far we have breath, presence, meditation, rest, and water. These are such seemingly basic parts of daily living it's easy to see why they can slip into the backdrop as no big deal. Most of us, if we are fortunate enough to have access to clean water, just drink water without even thinking.

You may not be like me but I was never a big water drinker. Fluids for me primarily came through coffee and a couple of weird phases where I drank a lot of energy drinks. I just didn't have much attention on water let alone how much I was or wasn't consuming. The truth is water is one of the most revitalizing health assets we can benefit from. There are some great books written on it. One of my favorites is *Your Body's Many Cries For Water; You're Not Sick You're Thirsty Don't Treat Thirst with Medication* by F. Batmanghelidj, M.D., if you'd like to gain a deeper understanding of the power of water. In short, when we are dehydrated it doesn't always show up as thirst.

Especially if we're consuming other fluids beyond just water. Dehydration can be the culprit of many adverse effects we experience throughout a day that we might not ever associate with not drinking enough water. It makes sense to many of us to drink enough water when we are sweating and working out, engaged in physical activity but it turns out that our mental and emotional energy exerted throughout a day desperately needs far more water to run smoothly. Side effects of not drinking enough water can be but are not limited to:

- Irritability
- Fogginess
- Body aches
- Bloating
- Fatigue
- Low energy
- Digestive issues

I would have thought these symptoms might only show up for someone out in the desert dying of thirst. But lo and behold, I was someone who had been very dehydrated for a long time. I spent an abundance of time with my grandma growing up and she was a spitfire, old school, classy, and very vocally opinionated. I respected that trait more and more about her as I got older realizing she'd been a positive influence on how internally referenced I am. She point-blank said, "I don't like water. Never have, never will and I'm fine without it." She stayed true to her word and Grandma drank coffee, milk, and occasionally a soda. It would suffice to say that looking back I can see clearly how hard being dehydrated was on her body and mind. Had I had more information I might have been able to out-stubborn-her to start drinking water. After, I began staying hydrated--it's day and night. I even look younger, a fun side benefit.

FOOD.

I don't want to say a lot about food. Primarily because so much has been and is being said about food and much of the information is overwhelmingly conflicting. There are some fundamentals that hold true despite any eating regimen you're on. My sister, Heather Davis, is an RN and health expert. She owns a company called Feed Your Cells. (I'm really pressuring her to write a book because she's brilliant). She uses the term whole-food-plant-based on a regular basis. Instead of focusing on high-protein, low carb, calories, macro, etc. shift your focus to increasing your whole-food-plant-based consumption and your body and your energy will love you for it. If possible, do organic when you can. We've made food so much about body shape and size that the topic of nutrients that the body needs to optimally function gets buried in the background.

NATURE.

Oh sweet nature. I grew up in the mountains in a small town in Colorado. The air was clean, the views of the mountain ridges were breathtaking, and every color and every season brought forth something new and beautiful... and I took it for granted. I knew it was beautiful every now and then. Mostly when I looked out over fresh snow with no tracks and the earth just looked covered in a white soft blanket. Fall. A paintbrush filled with every color would sweep over the land. The aspen trees were my favorite--turning bright yellow and orange.

It took me moving to LA at 18 years old, venturing off to college to really understand the stark contrast between the feel of a cement city and a nature-rich environment. It took me until my 30s to understand just how powerful taking a simple walk outside in nature really is. I heard someone call the trees "the standing people" not too long ago and for some reason I just loved that. They said if you go and rest up against a tree it will always offer you support, more than just physically.

Honestly, it doesn't matter what your belief system or how you see nature the powerful healing effect of being in nature is undeniable. I can't tell you how many times I was stuck in my head with tension coursing through my body and the last thing I felt like I had time to do was go take a walk. After forcing myself to do it and feeling better every single time, I decided something that yields a 100% success rate in positive results is worth continuing. Today, I feel very connected to nature. I've collected rocks since I was a little girl, I think I've always been connected to nature I just wasn't aware of it. We all are.

MOVEMENT.

Intentional and judgment-free movement. Our bodies love to move. Ironically, when we're feeling tired, sore, and burnt-out, movement often brings us up. It's so counterintuitive- when we least want to move- might be the best time to do it. Like food, movement has also been chained to body shape and size. It has been reduced to a means to an end. Instead of an end in and of itself. For example, dancing for a couple minutes in your living room can bring such joy, freedom, and invigoration. But someone might not do it, even if they felt like it because they might think "what's a few minutes of dancing going to do for me? I feel silly, plus it won't make a difference whether I do or don't because it's not like I'm going to lose weight with a few minutes of dancing." What if when you felt like dancing for a few minutes you just gave yourself permission to dance for a few minutes just because it made you feel good? That's intentional, intuitive, and judgment-free.

Taking short walks or long walks, running or stretching, swimming or rollerblading, riding your bike or doing tai chi, or just standing up at your desk and stretching your arms towards the ceiling-will make you feel better. Intentional and judgment-free movement creates enough space for you to start listening to your own body intuitively. It's here to help you and vice versa and often it tells us what it needs. We have a hard time listening because we've moved our purpose for moving so far outside of ourselves that often it takes our body screaming at us through injury or illness for us to listen.

Our body is like our conduit between our thoughts, our actions and much of the internal activation that takes place is influenced by the emotions we hold or allow ourselves to express. Our bodies are the connection point between the physical as we understand it and the non-physical

Movement is such a powerful part of what keeps us optimally navigating our internal and external world. When we have a surge of emotions or feel that tension is building up inside or aches and pains are emerging, giving yourself permission to move without judgment can transform almost any experience that you're in.

Feel
Your
Feelings

Categorize the fundamentals I just mentioned.
Which are you doing?
Which are you ignoring?
Why?

_____

_____

_____

_____

_____

_____

_____

_____

_____

_____

_____

_____

You're Not An Imposter

7

YOU'RE NOT AN IMPOSTER

As I stood on the red circle, the stage lights in my eyes, I could still see the thousand-plus, crowd stretching out in front of me. Seated, staring, waiting for me to speak. I was possibly the most nervous I have ever been before going on stage and speaking to a crowd. Being asked to speak at a TedX conference was an honor and truly something I'd hoped to have the opportunity to do someday. When I was initially asked, I was so excited and grateful with just a touch of *I don't deserve this*, lurking. Then as I begin to narrow in on what "idea worth spreading" I'd like to share over the following few months, prior to the talk, I found myself questioning everything about me.

I wanted to talk about the idea that it was a form of selfishness, not selflessness to not go after your dreams. I have done so much research and studying around the mind and the positive effects that occur for the individual and the collective when we honor who we really are and do what we love. I believed then and I believe even more now--going after your dreams is one of our greatest contributions to humanity. It became very clear to me, especially scientifically, playing small serves no one. I felt passionate about the topic and extremely excited to share it, practiced and felt great about it.

One week prior almost to the day, I began to panic. I felt confident about the subject matter. Experientially, I had the authority to speak and share on the topic. I was mid-PhD, I had some very successful business ventures under my belt, and had an extremely transformational couple of years behind me, a lifetime of stories, and I was writing my first book. There I stood one week before and thought *who in the hell do I think I am to do this TEDx talk*? Suddenly, I felt I hadn't practiced enough and the glaring bigger issue that didn't feel like I was enough. An intense feeling of being an imposter crept in and became louder as the day on the red circle neared.

There I stood alone on stage gripped with the idea that *I shouldn't be here*. On top of everything, I was the first person to go in the lineup. If you know anything about speaking to a crowd--they're not warm yet, meaning they're still adjusting and settling in. When I'm not feeling like I'm an imposter that's actually one of my favorite places to meet an audience, I love to get them feeling welcomed and engaged. Today, I was terrified that I shouldn't be there. I finally begin to speak after what felt like forever. I should also add that I was speaking where I lived, Modesto, California, which was filled with many people that I knew. Possibly people involved in my perfect-shit-storm time who may or may not believe I should be there as well. This was just gasoline on my fire - believing that I did not belong.

As I'm talking, somehow, in the sea of over a thousand people, lights that made it difficult to really identify anyone's faces past the first few rows (maybe it was my nerves), I see clearly the looks on a few peoples faces that I know and two were smiling and one with the "you definitely don't belong here" look on her face. She was slowly shaking her head with a disconcerting look. *My God*, for a brief second I forgot what I was going to say next. I kept going.

My eyes trail and way out in the crowd I recognize a family of four. They had only met me and known me at my worst. I was their neighbor while I was going through a divorce. Ugh. Trust me, they did not see the best side of me and I hadn't seen them for years. I imagine it was a hard leap in their mind from Erica that was having a life crisis to Erica who was standing on the TedX stage giving a talk about the imperativeness of following your dreams. I actually saw them leaning over each other to talk with the looks of surprise and pointing. I may have imagined this but it felt like disapproval. *I can't even…* I managed to get through it and I even had this thought in the middle *if I can do this now and stand, then I can do this anywhere* and that gave me the strength to keep going and finish.

I should also add on a funny side note that my husband Brad, who believes in me with all of his heart, told me later that he could tell that I was struggling when I was up there and he was so nervous for me, the second he thought I had finished he wanted to kick off the clapping in support of me. What he didn't realize was that I wasn't quite finished when he began clapping. We had a great laugh about it. I was just so thankful to be done. I had some strong mixed emotions following that talk. It was by far not the best job I've ever done but I will give myself a 10 for courage and perseverance. Did I really deserve to be there that day? *Was I really enough* was more closely the question. I was sincerely asking myself- *was I an imposter*? And if I was, what more did I need to be so that I wasn't an imposter? And if I wasn't an imposter than why did I feel like one?

Definition of imposter according to Merriam-Webster: one that assumes a false identity or title for the purpose of deception.

Let's dig in.

Have you ever felt like an imposter? Like you weren't sure if you really belong or deserve to be wherever you are? I noticed an interesting pattern. I would start feeling more like an imposter as my level of success increased. Confusing. Being an entrepreneur for the last 20 years, you can bet that I've successfully and unsuccessfully embarked on many business adventures.

Here's what I noticed-- every new thing I would start I would begin feeling uncertain and nervous about my learning curve. I would dominantly be concerned about what skills I needed to further develop to do a great job. What new systems do I need to create or implement to make everything run smoothly? What are the ins and outs of the industry? What is my target market? What are the products and services we're offering? Financials, overhead, profit margins, projections, taxes--the many things that establish a successful business.

It's always hard initially starting because I would feel terribly unconfident until I learned what I needed to learn and put everything into practice. Over time I would gain confidence that I could get the job done. However, at the beginning of each venture, I would have this small little voice in the back of my head that would say; *You shouldn't be here. You don't know what you're doing. Who do you think you are? You're going to screw this up.* This was tough to hear but it would be subtle in the backdrop of my daily actions and goals towards whatever I was trying to accomplish. *But* as I became more and more confident about the logistics of the actual job that I was doing that little voice whispering *you're just not good enough* would start to get louder. In fact, it was the loudest during my greatest accomplishments.

This became very clear when I analyzed what the heck happened leading up to and during the TedX talk. This was confusing to say the least. At the time, I hadn't really connected those dots. As I really allowed myself to go into some self-exploration and find out more about what was going on inside me, this idea of me feeling like an imposter seemed to be a theme. I was able to look back and see that something similar took place inside of me during my personal bigger moments. I carried this unwavering sense that I just didn't belong.

It began to start making sense as I really sat with it. When I was struggling to learn something new, emphasis on the word struggling, that matched more how I saw myself. Struggling. I was more comfortable scrutinizing the things I could've done better and still needed improvement on, you know-getting better but not quite there – still room for improvement. I also realized that much of how I saw myself was through the framework of my past mistakes. It was like deep in my subconscious belief system I thought that because *I'm not perfect, I don't deserve to truly see myself as a really successful person.* I suppose deep down it was always this lingering belief- *If people really knew how much I've struggled they would see me as a failure and I would be found out.* I had filtered every milestone of progress through the lens of I am not enough therefore I'm an imposter. The things that proved to me in my mind that I wasn't enough were:

COMPARISON. I would see how someone else was doing and have this picture in my mind that they weren't struggling. Clearly, truly successful people didn't have a train wreck of emotions going on inside of them. Therefore that's a person that's enough, not me. I've since discovered we all feel like emotional train wrecks at some point. It just takes courage to admit it.

MISTAKES. I've made many mistakes. Outwardly, I would tell you that I understood mistakes were a natural part of growing and that everybody makes mistakes. That's true and rational. Deep down, I wasn't OK with me making mistakes. My mistakes seemed bigger and worse than what was acceptable. Now, mind you these aren't beliefs that I was conscious of and able to talk about like I am right now. In the midst of it I just had this bad feeling that I would push away.

It wasn't until I started really looking into what information I was using to decide for myself if I was enough. As I let my mind become curious about what I really believed about making mistakes, I saw and felt it: *other people can make mistakes but not me.* I couldn't afford the mistakes because of something even deeper. *Something is wrong with me.* When I got way in there and felt it I just really believed that something was wrong with me. I felt I had evidence to prove it. *Bad things happened to me because something was wrong with me and bad things happened to my family and I couldn't fix it. People that I felt that I could trust had betrayed me.*

I had been physically and emotionally violated at different points in my life. Part of me believed that these things happened because something was really wrong with me. No matter what I did or what I achieved or how well I performed and how few mistakes I tried to make this poor belief about who I really was laid underneath it all. Informing the measuring stick that I judged my life against. I defined myself by. No amount of external affirmation or personal achievement could shake what I had decided was true so long ago. I'm not enough because something is fundamentally wrong with me. The more successful I would become, the more this belief would be challenged and come flying up to the surface. *If your successful it's because you've fooled everyone.*

The tentacles of this belief reached far and wide for me. No matter how trained professionally I became, nothing could outweigh my internal comparison and the fundamental flaw I believed about me. Even as I write this, I realize how dramatic it sounds and rides the line teetering between rational and irrational. I can see how I came to those conclusions but on the same note when you write them down or say them out loud... it sounds so serious. Well, that's because it is and it was seriously wreaking havoc on my life experience. I was only able to see and let all this go after I had been willing to feel. The second we ask a tough question and a tough feeling shows up-if we can't sit there long enough to receive an answer then we can change anything.

I seemed to attract so many people and circumstances that would reinforce this imposter thing. In my, *I Am* book, I went in-depth on why and how this works. Let me just say, if critics were sharks and I was swimming in the ocean-- this belief about not feeling good enough-- blood in the water. I mean *of course*, during the TedX talk, I would lock eyes with probably the one person in the crowd that thought the least of me, seriously what are the chances?

This feeling that I'm not enough and that, somehow, I'm an imposter pretending to be someone who is and pretending that I deserve to be here - deceiving all the people that think well of me-- had to go. Many people feel the same way. Some of the most "successful" people throughout history had the same struggle. Even recently, I read Shonda Rhimes's book, *The Year of Yes!*, and she said she felt similar. Shonda was not a troublemaker growing up, knew what she wanted to do from the time she was young, worked her butt off and graduated top of her class at Dartmouth University, and has since become one of the single most powerful television producers, creators. Two of her shows hold the most coveted slots on television. *And* she felt unsure if she deserved to be where she was.

So who is exempt from this sense of impostorism? Maybe small children before any other kids or grownups say the dumb things we say with our good or not so good intentions? I say that only half facetiously. Seriously, if astronauts, presidents, and some of the world's greatest leaders have fought off feelings of being an imposter, it begs the question, is it possible to truly not feel like one and if so how?

Yes and no and yes. It's like a shit sandwich for most of us. Good news, bad news, good news. Good news: Yes it's possible to not feel like an imposter the vast majority of the time including but not limited to hitting extremely important milestones. Bad news: No, it's probably not possible to never question your worth or right to be here again. Good news: It is possible to be able to recognize and breeze through feeling like an imposter so it doesn't leave you on stage feeling like a jerk. Or steal your thunder every time something great happens for you. The moral of the story is: it doesn't matter how we came to feel like we're not enough, which results in feeling like an imposter.

The only thing that really matters now is recognizing it and doing something new moving forward. As we've already said at length you can't help the feelings or stop feelings from coming out, they just come up. You can mitigate the number of rough feelings you have coming up by paying more attention to what you're thinking and slowly change the trajectory of your thought life (the origin for most of our emotions). But even thoughts pop into your head without permission or warning much of the time and as we can see many are consciously unrecognized. So this leaves us with navigating our emotions differently as they arise giving ourselves enough space to see what's going on and take full responsibility for changing it.

This doesn't mean that I'm not going to have moments of panic. However, I've allowed myself to sit with what I truly believe about me and not run from all of the billowing emotions of insecurity, shame, and anger surrounding my perceived value. I came to a realization by way of logic. Nothing I have achieved, nor any amount of outside affirmation has ever been able to truly move the needle regarding my personal value. I have been measuring myself against a measuring stick that I created with my own thoughts and beliefs. Nothing outside of me can fix this. As the saying goes, if it's to be, it's up to me. So ironically, this debate was not going to be resolved in my favor by kicking more ass at life.

This was going to have to be a decision that I and I alone had to make for myself internally. I would need to be my own accountability partner in making this change of belief. Further, it would be entirely up to me to be vigilant in noticing when the thoughts, feelings, or beliefs surrounding the issue come up. It would then also be me who would need to allow myself to feel the feelings I was having and without condemnation remind myself of my decision: *I am enough and I am not an imposter.*

Further, knowing it's OK if sometimes I feel like I'm not enough, feeling that way doesn't make it true. If this sounds like a lot of work to self-monitor on this level then may I remind you of the work you have already grown accustomed too. If you have dealt with even a fraction of what I have regarding avoiding how you feel or feeling like you're not enough then you know managing that rodeo is an all-day everyday full-time job. It takes extreme amounts of energy, focus, and determination to actively and regularly try to avoid shitty feelings. May I also remind you that the payoff for all of that work is exhaustion, depression, anxiety, constant fear, a droning sense of nervousness, etc.

The cherry on top of avoiding how you feel is suppressed joy, pleasure, happiness, and low-level satisfaction. Side effects are funky ways to find pleasure:

- Using food by over or under eating.
- Financial issues from overspending or obsessing about every dollar spent.
- Personal relationships. Enough said.
- Health issues, including but not limited to all the things caused by stress which is pretty much, on some level, every disease. I am obviously not a medical doctor so feel free to ask your doctor how stress correlates with the emergence of disease in the body and molecular and cellular health.
- Legacy issues. It is difficult if not impossible to not lead by example with our children. Do as I say, not as I do is actually code for *I have no idea what I'm doing*. We alternately are all on our own journey. Wouldn't it be nice to know your child

would feel equipped to navigate their internal world as well as their external world? Wouldn't it be wonderful to know that your child would never break because they already mastered the art of bending? To master your mind is to master your destiny.

Honestly, the list could go on and on. The repercussions of walking around feeling like an imposter, that we're not enough, and avoiding how we feel will translate into living a much smaller existence than you meant to. We all desire to feel that we belong with certainty, to know that we are enough and we deserve to be here, wherever that here is for you. The only way to have certainty regarding the above is to decide. Make the decision that you are enough and that you're not an imposter.

As children, we were told what to do often like "sit down" and if we didn't know how to sit down. it could be demonstrated by the other person sitting down. Now, what if someone, a parent, teacher, or a mentor says "calm down" or "change your attitude" or "Believe in yourself". Could anyone show you? I mean really show you what they did on the inside to calm down, change their attitude, make it a happy day, believe in themselves? No, they would've really had to break it down to you and maybe some of you had someone that was able to talk about all of these things in-depth and really help you navigate but chances are you didn't.

Again, we can't teach what we don't know how to do. Most people don't know how they calm down. They're not sure how they came to believe in themselves, they just do. The internal world isn't visible and it doesn't occur to most young kids to ask about it? How exactly do I believe in myself? It just lands in one of those categories where we just hope and pray that we will all just intuitively know what to do. If you think about what we've been talking about we might intuitively know many of these things but that would require consciously listening to our intuition versus reacting.

The reason I am going so far in this direction for a minute is to help layout the rational explanation for why we don't know what the hell is going on inside of us nor what to do with it. In a way, it's like a skill that many of us just haven't learned yet maybe because we didn't even know that we really could learn it or that it matters. Especially when talking about emotion, it's typically framed with derogatory or judgmental inflection.

- "Don't make it an emotional decision."
- "That person is an emotional wreck."
- "Get your emotions in check."

I mean do you ever hear someone say "that person is a thinking wreck"? Emotion has generally been presented as a weakness. Period. The topic of Emotional Intelligence is peeking its way into the culture. Even though that "weakness" is one of the most powerful drivers of the human experience for better or worse and there is absolutely no opt-out checkbox of feeling. You can either learn to harness the transformative power of your emotions or be blindly driven and chased by them.

The great news is we get to decide and we can start at the very next moment we take a breath. We don't need any more schooling, you don't have to spend any more money, we don't have to overhaul our life to start mastering our internal world. When we stop running, we're no longer afraid of our own emotional shadow and instead make room. When we know that we can handle anything that comes up inside of us without reacting outside of our own best interest we start to feel incredibly empowered. When we feel like we can handle our own emotions without suppressing them, we certainly have the courage to ask ourselves really difficult questions like what the heck happened to me during the Tedx talk and further, we can actually hear the answer from our intuition and clear mind without all the noise. We can choose differently with our eyes wide open. The next thing you know, you'll realize you've always been enough. You just hadn't decided yet. You didn't realize you had a choice to make and once you really decide-- you'll feel like you belong with certainty.

Feel
Your
Feelings

Have you ever felt like an imposter?
Like you weren't sure if you really belong or
deserve to be wherever you are?
Describe the experience.

_____

_____

_____

_____

_____

_____

_____

_____

_____

_____

_____

Lemonade Stand

8

LEMONADE STAND

When life gives you lemons--open a lemonade stand. At least in my opinion. Each of us have interests that we naturally gravitate toward, technology, painting, teaching, athletics, cooking, health, the list is really endless. Here's what I've noticed about myself and others. We all seem to function the best when we are doing something we love with the majority of our time. I mean really honoring who you are as a person.

Now let's get this out-of-the-way right out front. When I say doing what you love the majority of the time, what I really mean is you are willing to *do what it takes* to get to do what you love the majority of the time. Doing what you love, aligning your life to reflect what matters most to you, helps you do everything you came here to do. This is helpful to everyone. There are a few things that I believe stop people dead in their tracks from going after what they really want in life.

The lemons. People are pissed, hurt, tired and afraid. The lemons were too upsetting. The person they loved left them. The people they trusted burned them. The investment fell through. Something deeply tragic happened to them or someone close to them. They put it all on the line and lost. Whatever form the lemons came in, they were sour and we didn't want them. So moving forward, they consciously or unconsciously pull back from hoping too much, being too excited and get as far away from risk as possible.

These are the purple hearts. They sacrifice everything that could've really created a fulfilling life to avoid the pain of really living it. They will work at a job that they hate all the way through to retirement. They will stay in a relationship no matter how unhealthy or unfulfilling. They will do the same thing day in and day out and not sincerely question the monotony. They may be miserable on the inside and may or may not show it on the outside but either way, they feel stuck with their lemons.

———

The lemonade. Fine. Crazy shit happened it hurt a lot, I barely got back up but I did and I'm going to move forward with these lemons and make lemonade. But the lemonade was a lot of work. Squeezing lemon juice burns my hands. It's too time-consuming to try to get it to really taste right. Besides deep down, I didn't ask for these lemons. To be honest, I'm still freaked out and I don't know if I want to put this much work in trying to make something good from something so sour. I think I'll just make a little lemonade every now and then. I'll work on it when I have enough energy and just really feel like doing it. These are the dabblers. They might make declarations of change to themselves or others but when it gets tough, their back to their lemons.

———

Then there are *the lemonade stand owners.*

This is what's possible with every batch of lemons. The more lemons you have, the bigger your lemonade stand can be. You can set up the biggest and best lemonade stand around. The lemonade stand represents truly making the most out of your life experiences. It represents making space for what you never asked for and allowing it to evolve you into the best version of yourself. It's seeing everything that comes to you as a possible resource to, ultimately, help you do more for yourself and others. It takes work and commitment. It takes a firm decision internally to filter all of life's perceived problems through this abundant lens.

With each perceived problem we must ask ourselves: What is the message? What is the resource that I now have because of what I've experienced? How can I use this to better my life and the lives of those around me? This creates true resourcefulness and abundance. Nothing then happens in vain leaving a residue of bitterness. The problems of today can become the fertilizer for tomorrow and grow the garden that provides the food for the whole village in the future. It's a balance between living in the moment while maintaining a focus on long-term future potentials.

If you can do this you will always come out on top. You won't find yourself stuck holding lemons and pissed off at the world. You won't see it as a burden to make lemonade but an opportunity for good. You can stay in your power. Life is happening for you not to you. You can generate a lemonade stand that will create so much more for you and others on a continual basis. These are the change-makers. They are not just pushed by life but pulled by creating compelling possibilities.

———

Some people get paid to do what they love and some people get paid and do what they love. Both routes can bring about a truly fulfilling life and both of them require intentionality.

If you want to get *paid to do what you love to do,* you have to let yourself really get clear on the biggest problem you would love to help solve for others. This doesn't require you to be the best problem solver of whatever the problem is, it just requires you to truly be able to solve the problem effectively for someone. Think about what problem would bring you the most joy to solve? Just because you can doesn't mean you should.

Would you love to wake up and help people solve that problem every day? Are you passionate about it? Are you willing to learn the necessary skills that you may need to learn to do it even more effectively? Generally speaking when you can find a way to make a profit from what brings you passion and purpose then you have found your sweet spot. Then you need to decide if you want to do this inside of someone else's company or start your own. This also plays into getting paid to do what you love. Not everyone wants to own their own business. For some, owning your own business was factored into part of doing what you love and getting paid for it. It is important to make the distinction between whether you want to be an entrepreneur or a valuable member of a companies team.

I've been an entrepreneur for nearly two decades. At some point, I realized that I was made for it. I'm passionate about every aspect of building a successful company. I love helping people with the companies that I own. Being an entrepreneur has helped me immensely in navigating my internal world mainly because it has challenged me to my core at various times and I had to look inside to evolve myself. Owning your own business can be one of the most fulfilling, creative, exciting adventures one can go on. The other side of the coin is that it can be filled with massive amounts of uncertainty and extremely high levels of responsibility for yourself and many others. This may not appeal to everyone. If you choose to be a valued member on someone's team doing something that you love, you can have all the benefits of passion and purpose while making a profit with less uncertainty and pressure.

The best route to choose is the one that resonates the most with you. Both take work internally and externally and both can create a fantastic lemonade stand.

Some people get paid to do something they don't

necessarily love but it affords them the freedom to do what they love outside of work. The distinction here is that maybe their job isn't very fulfilling but ideally they don't hate it. But it provides the financial freedom to be able to intentionally create a life that brings them fulfillment and joy. Outside of work, it is important to align your life with what brings you passion and purpose and it's OK to keep your profits separate as long as what you do for work is not sucking the life out of you. You can also use the "grow where you're planted" concept. While your job may not be very fulfilling, you can use it to consciously and intentionally evolve you by looking for ways to grow. This can be very fulfilling. Outside of work, it is important for us to really design our lives intentionally. When you think about how easy it is for us to accidentally live in Groundhog's Day for no other reason than to avoid the emotions of change or uncertainty, it explains how we can accidentally let a decade pass without making much progress in the life fulfillment category.

Creating an intentional life that allows you to do what you love can take a lot of work. First, there's physical work. This can vary, obviously, from person to person depending on their goals. If you've got big goals then you have to be willing to put in big work. But even small goals require consistent and daily effort. The real work that can radically change the experience of everything in your life is, yes you guessed it, the internal work. If you can handle your emotions in a way that creates a place for you to be fully human then you'll get much further, faster with a lot less damage.

Here's a great example of this. Just the other day, I had a friend tell me he had just lost two of his largest clients that generated the majority of his company's revenue. It was a big hit financially. He could have said, "I'm fine, I'm just going to get more clients" and acted like a badass phased by nothing. Instead, he said, "I feel utterly devastated right now, like I'm really questioning if I have what it takes to make this company successful. That hit me so hard that my chest hurts." And I thought, *wow, now that is a real badass*. I watched him take deep breathes and feel all the stuff coming up.

At that moment, I knew that he absolutely had what it took to not only make his company succeed but make his life succeed. He was so honest with himself about how he really felt he was able to move forward quickly and wasn't carrying any of that frantic sprinter, run from your emotions. energy. He was able to bounce forward calmly and empowered making strong decisions with effective problem-solving without having to waste any energy on suppressing the experience. He actually grew exponentially through it instead of retracting. This is what it takes to really do life beneficially as a human being.

Being afraid or ashamed of how we really feel only de-optimizes our full potential. Our willingness to feel the painful emotions will equal our ability to feel the great ones. It is far better to sit down and acknowledge you feel like shit or your heart feels broken or you worried your failing- and let that work through your body without suppressing it than to say, "Nope, I'm fine" and brush it off. There's no such thing as brushing off your feelings.

They just stack up on your desk waiting to acknowledged now or 50 years from now. If you want a thriving lemonade stand where life only moves you forward and problems are opportunities to guide you on your best life- then it's time to stop running.

Feel
Your
Feelings

Let's be honest!
How do you deal with lemons?
Describe the pattern of behavior.

9

You're Either In or Out

YOU'RE EITHER IN OR OUT

It's hard to un-see what you have already seen. As I became open to learning more information about how we work as humans- specifically how I work- it became increasingly difficult to not want to go deeper. When I came to understand how powerful my thoughts and emotions were and to what degree they were informing my life experience through my patterns of behavior I became obsessed in the best way possible. I became willing to do, be, or learn whatever was necessary so that I would stop running into so many walls. It really resonated with me that we are truly sovereign beings connected to something greater than ourselves, separate yet completely connected.

When I began to clearly see the thoughts that were running through my mind on a regular basis and sit with the feelings of uncomfortability without running, I started to feel strength and hope like never before. It was like having access to a treasure map that I could choose to use or not use right there inside of me. The treasure was my freedom. Freedom from running with the ability to engage with the present moment. The freedom to create and live the life I really love waking up in.

This doesn't mean that I feel happy all the time or even free all of the time, in fact, I have some really rough feeling days. But the difference today--I don't get stuck. I don't go backward and I don't shrink. I have the ability to feel like total shit and still win. I don't panic about feeling bad I just think *Yep I'm having a lot of rough emotions pumping through me* and I just breathe through it. Sometimes I meditate. Sometimes I cry. Sometimes I'll talk to someone about how I'm feeling. Sometimes I'll just sit there and do nothing. I'll tell you what I don't do anymore. I don't worry about having tough moments.

I haven't talked about this earlier in the book because I didn't want it to be a focal point but it's definitely worth talking about. Every single one of us has overwhelming feelings that come up as we've discussed at length. When we lose the fear of feeling, something unstoppable awakens. I just know that I can handle feeling anything good or bad and that both come and go and that's living. However, I do deal with something pretty intense every month that has given me the opportunity to truly practice what I preach so to speak.

One week each month, somewhere between five and six days, occasionally closer to ten days, all of my happy feelings, hopeful and optimistic feelings vanish completely. During this time, brushing my teeth or getting out of bed feels like an enormous amount of work. During this time, sounds feel much louder and lights seem much brighter but not in a good way. I will basically have a steady stream of thoughts that hold the theme: *you're not OK your life is falling apart and you're not gonna make it.* I have something called PMDD. I believe I've had it since I was about eight or nine years old. I started my premenstrual cycle when I was eight which is young but not unheard of. PMDD has often been misdiagnosed as clinical depression or bipolar disorder. It mimics similar symptoms but it presents 12-4 days approximately before the start of each monthly menstruation cycle. It is absolutely, 100% not to be confused with PMS. If PMS is a speed bump, PMDD is a brick wall. They have completely different pathologies. Here is a condensed explanation of PMDD from the scientific advisory board for the largest clinical trial study on PMDD.

"PMDD is a severe hormonal condition triggered by the steroid allopregnanolone. It is not a mental illness. It is far more severe than typical PMS. It is a biological, not a behavioral, condition. PMDD symptoms are cyclical— and debilitating: They build up in the two weeks before a period (the luteal phase), peak in the week directly before, and then recede quickly when the period starts. Emotional symptoms: extreme mood swings, severe irritability and/or anger, depression, feelings of hopelessness and low self-worth (women with PMDD are four times more likely to attempt suicide), anxiety, feeling overwhelmed and out of control, difficulty concentrating." (www.asarinaPharma.com/pmdd/)

The world's first effective treatment for PMDD is expected to be released 2022-2025. If you or someone you care about wants to understand PMDD in much greater detail visit www.asarinapharma.com for the most accurate and advanced information I have found in my research. They are based in Sweden with trials in Sweden, Poland, Germany, and the UK.

I know this sounds wild but I was unable to connect the dots between the devastating feelings occurring right before I'd begin my monthly for 25 years. To be frank, the feelings were so severe that it didn't seem possible that my period had anything to do with it. All of the women I knew or had heard of maybe had irritability, fatigue or maybe severe cramping prior to their menstruation. No one I knew hit debilitating feelings of hopelessness accompanied by an inability to concentrate. I was 33 years old when I made the correlation. I also made the connection that the only time I would excessively consume alcohol was during that same time. I was 35 when a research center in Sweden made massive headway on understanding the pathology of PMDD and began phase 2 trials of the first promising treatment. PMDD affects 1 in 20 women. Many have been miss diagnosed with Bipolar Disorder or Clinical Depression and are potentially on medication for an inaccurate diagnosis.

Why am I sharing all of this with you now? I want you to know you're not trapped no matter what you're facing. I could literally have a problem-free life and once a month a light switch goes off and I lose the ability to "feel happy" in fact I am flooded with extremely tough emotions and so much more. My ability to be metacognitive (see what I'm thinking and notice what I'm feeling) has saved my life. I can hormonally lose my ability to feel pleasure and be hit with a flood of hopeless thoughts and emotions and I can get right through it. I feel them, notice them, and chose my response. Calmly and from an empowered place. I am the master of my mind and my emotions. I don't need to suppress them or run from them, I make space for them and keep powerfully creating my life. I don't need to wait for anything outside of myself to make me feel better, healthy or whole. We are the freedom we seek.

I'm sharing this to let you know what I'm talking about really works. I am a living example of what's possible. I have an ability today to have a weeklong uncontrollable flood of the worst possible thoughts and emotions you can imagine run through me and I am able to respond without panicking, self-destructing or disconnecting from my family. Remember my Tedx Talk? That landed on my PMDD week. There have been many things in my career that felt 100 times more overwhelming with PMDD involved but I finally had to make room for it. I used to feel so ashamed. I thought that if I were strong enough or high conscious enough I could make it go away. Every time it came, which is every single month, I would spend a week pouring shame gasoline on the already intense fire and the following week more shame, combined with scary perfectionist energy.

The truth is it comes suddenly and it happens to me each month. Someday it might not but I don't need it to stay or go to be my best self or live my best life. I just need to be where I am and create life one fresh moment at a time. I have created more with less "effort" than ever before with this approach. I hope in sharing this you might be encouraged that no matter what you're up against it's possible to really and truly be free.

Feel
Your
Feelings

How do you deal with routinely uncontrollable situations? Experiences that knock you out of balance even though you know they're coming? It could be having to visit a relative or a recurring medical condition. What is your reaction? If you could craft your response, what would that look like?

It's Ok
To Be
Polarizing.

10

IT'S OK TO BE POLARIZING

I want to help everybody. I want everyone to like me. I
don't want to offend anyone. I don't want to exclude
anyone. I'm afraid that if I'm true to myself I'm going to
lose people?

When we look at these words in black and white, don't
we immediately see that it's impossible to please
everyone? None the less these are real concerns for many
people. No matter how irrational they may be, these were
definitely my concerns for a long time. As we discussed in
earlier chapters about not wanting to be rejected there can
be this temptation to try to be everything for everyone.
How many of us have heard things like:

- "You can't please everyone."
- "Not everyone's going to like you."
- "Anyone who does anything great is going to
  have critics."
- Or one of my favorite, "If you don't want to

> have critics say nothing, do nothing, be
> nothing."

Something tells me that even in that scenario there is still no way to avoid criticism. I personally had to completely re-frame how I viewed and experienced criticism. There are not two types of criticism, there are five types of critiques. At least this is how I've categorized them. You may have heard the terms constructive criticism and non-constructive criticism. In my experience, criticism can be useful. Getting clear on the *type of critic* can really help disengage any feelings of negativity that can come with criticism.

———

CRITIC #1: *The hater*. The hater hates their life and probably more specifically himself. Some may come off as arrogant and confident and some may come off as openly insecure or bitter. Either way, the hater's intention through their criticism is not to build someone up but to tear someone down. It's not as much about what they're saying, it's where they're coming from when they say it.

Trying to please a hater is a fool's errand. Their problem isn't actually with you, it's with themselves. Even if you took time out of your life to engage with them and attempt to help them see something in a different light or see things from their point with the intention of understanding. It's a waste of your power and energy. As quickly as you put out one fire, your hater will start another the very next day.

Haters are going to hate as long as they hate themselves. They can't help it. When they're coming from a place of insecurity about themselves and their life, criticizing or hating on others is one of their only ways to make themselves feel better. So when you're trying to tell a hater to stop hating, you're essentially asking them to take away one of the few things that temporarily makes them feel better. They would have to take a lot of internal personal steps to get to a place where they were willing to see what was really going on with them to make any lasting change.

So unless you want to become their psychologist, it's far better to step back, do your thing and let haters hate. Every time I see someone criticizing another (including me) with clearly no good intention, I just think to myself, *I'm sorry you're so unhappy with yourself.* Again it's not what a critic says, it's the intention and energy behind what they're saying. It reeks of negativity and we can just walk around that pothole.

––––––

CRITIC # 2: *The know it all.* This person can often go either way. Sometimes they can be really constructive and sometimes they go straight down a rabbit hole. They honestly believe they know it all. They're not secretly thinking, "I really don't know it all. I just want to be really annoying. I have no desire to learn anything beyond what I already know." No. It's more simple, they feel right and you're wrong. So they're not necessarily coming with a negative intention to hurt you they really just believe with all their heart they already know and they're letting you know the "right" way to see it so you're not misguided.

Occasionally, it's worth the debate. Occasionally you can learn some really cool things from know-it-alls. But either way if you find yourself trying to change the viewpoint of a know it all, you may find that they have the stamina to outlast you. You have to remember it's not a give-and-take conversation. God help you if it's someone with a few letters behind their name. They're going to give you the right answer and if you want to get along with them then you better take it. Again, it just comes back to you if you're up for the energy spend. It can feel life sucking so personally I steer clear. I'm only open to genuine two-way conversations. I don't have time for closed minds/hearts or monologues.

———

CRITIC # 3: *The fool*. They are almost not worth mentioning. However, it's important to make this distinction. A hater can really get under your skin if you're not aware that it's really not about you. The hater might personally attack you and string together sentences that seem really thought out often with a jugular aim but nonetheless they may sound well-spoken. The fool, on the other hand, is the one-liner. Their attacks lack all depth and substance. You might hear things like you're ugly. Your hair looks bad. Or some other short negative profanity often with poor spelling and grammar. They don't spend a lot of time or energy piecing together their commentary. They still have to be mentioned because sometimes those can trigger the primal first-grader in us that wants to take it to heart and feel defensive. The truth is if you can really see this for what it is they actually become almost invisible to you.

———

CRITIC # 4: *The devil's advocate.* This can be constructive and useful. They are not looking for a heated debate nor do they want to harm you they just speak to the other side of the coin. This shouldn't create doubt in you or just curiosity. This can open the door to curiosity and possibly new insights for you. It's not about being right or wrong it's just something else to consider and decide for yourself if you want to integrate the information or leave it.

———

CRITIC #5: *The Conscious Critic.* True constructive feedback. This critic genuinely wants to help. They want to give you information about what they felt worked and didn't work in their opinion. If they're really helpful, they will even offer possible solutions to make your work better. They have given it honest thought and have no other intention other than to help you. And, again, it will always be up to you to sift and sort through what you would like to adjust or not adjust.

This is really the only critic worth your time and energy.

There's a fine line to balance on being open to feedback while simultaneously clear on what you were doing. Before we can deal effectively with criticism or feedback that's coming externally we have to have a come to Jesus with our own internal clinic.

Here are the rules, if you will, that I have established internally regarding my internal critic and how I view and engage with other critics:

1. There will always be someone who does not agree with what I'm doing or saying. With that in mind, it is imperative that I do and say what is true for me.

2. I don't need to be right or other people to be wrong. More than anything, I need to show up as the real me to be happy and healthy.

3. I am always open to feedback. I get to decide what feedback is worth my time and energy and I will use it to constructively to grow.

4. I can handle the feelings of being hurt, rejected, or disliked. It is a natural part of being willing to be seen.

5. For me to thrive in my human experience, I must accept myself. If I do or say things that cause me to not accept myself then I have chosen a path of suffering.

6. When I show up as me and say and do things that align with the real me, my tribe emerges. If I want to be surrounded by people that accept me for who I really am then I must not be afraid to be who I really am.

7. I trust the power of polarization. The people I attract are supposed to be there. The people I don't attract are not. I fully embrace this.

The definition of polarization is the division of sharply contrasting groups or sets of opinions or beliefs.

This is where people can get caught up or stuck. I had to ask myself an honest question and give an honest answer. Am I OK with people not agreeing with me? I was surprised by my answer. Initially, my answer was no. The reason this surprised me was because my rational mind understood that of course not everyone is going to agree with me so why would I hold an expectation that could never be met? I realized that it was 100% unrealistic. So then I asked myself why am I not OK with people disagreeing with me? My answer: Because if they don't agree with me then they're against me. Wow. Step back.

What am I a dictator? Looking at my personality, I'm more the person that wants everybody to get along and no one to be left out. I don't feel like a dictator. Maybe I'm a narcissist? Do I think my way is the only right way? Again, looking at my personality, no I'm very curious and open about all the different ways there are to get to the same destination. In fact, I've been accused of being too open because I firmly believe that everyone has their own way of seeing things. So then what on earth makes me say, *no I'm not OK with people not agreeing with me?*

Then I had the realization. I viewed opposite points of view as conflict and rejection. So it really wasn't that I truly needed people to agree with me it was the lens that I was viewing it through that needed to change. Having separate viewpoints did not mean conflict or rejection. It just meant separate viewpoints. When I saw it like that I truly stopped personalizing it with my old meaning. It took the crazy pressure off. Am I OK with people disagreeing with me today? Yes absolutely.

Become curious, not defensive. This really changes the playing field. Today, I approach feedback with curiosity, if it's the feedback that I've deemed worth my time and energy, I'll engage it. Curiosity opens the mind for new information to be seen. When we're on the defense, everything can quickly become distorted and we will only preserve what we already know. If you value personal growth as I do then you value learning above preserving.

Have you ever met someone that just knows what they know and are not open to knowing more? Like the know-it-all? They make a statement about something and you try to share some interesting information or new discovery about what they just said and they are defensive instead of curious? I wrote a lot in my first book about why we preserve what we already know. In short, it makes us feel safe and certain. And we know how feeling safe and certain keeps uncomfortable emotions at bay. So if you desire to be an open, growing, learning, person you have to be OK with not knowing so you can learn something new. This applies to critics and feedback. Feedback from surveys, friends, family, reviews can truly be priceless when you're drawing from what I am going to call conscious criticism.

Any criticism that's not conscious criticism always brings up this analogy for me: I love sports--playing them and watching them. It's always helped me understand criticism better. If I played football and I was out on the field in a game and I had someone screaming criticisms at me from the bleachers, here's what I would think.

How funny. I am training 6-7 days a week for hours crafting my skill, elevating my abilities, working my butt off to show up and withstand extreme pressure. I am playing with everything I've got for my teammates, for my family, and the people who backed me to get here. I am drenched in sweat. I'm exhausted, I'm getting my ass kicked and I'm getting right back up and giving it everything I've got. I will never quit and I will never stop trying to get better.

This out of shape person, drinking a beer, with ketchup on his shirt who works at God knows where, doing God knows what, is telling me what I'm doing wrong and that I suck. Seriously? If you would like to put some pads on and get your ass out on the field and show me that you're qualified to teach me something that will make me better then by all means. But if not, enjoy your peanuts at the peanut gallery.

If you haven't read Daring Greatly by Brene Brown, It's excellent. She writes about this passage from a speech given by Theodore Roosevelt called "The Man in the Arena". She makes the powerful point that the only people who have a right to say a damn thing to me are the people out in the arena with me. If you don't have dirt on your face and if your knees aren't bloody from getting your ass kicked from showing up and trying to give it everything you've got-- then be quiet in the cheap seats. Unless you're in the game - sit down and eat your hotdog.

Feel
Your
Feelings

Are you OK with people not agreeing with you?
How do you respond to criticism?

It's A Human Thing

11

IT'S A HUMAN THING

L et's do a fun little quiz. A little boy and a little girl both around 10 years old are made fun of while having a hard time reading out loud in school. Which one feels more shame? Which one is more embarrassed? Which one feels stupid? Which one feels like crying?

A grown man and a grown woman both separately own companies and are both around the age of 40. A major financial shift happens in their respective industries that cause them both to have to lay off their staff and close their business. They both spent the last two decades building their companies, taking care of their families, and everything they had was invested in making their company succeed.

Which one is sadder? Which one is more scared? Which one is angrier? Which one is more devastated? Which one feels more like they failed? Which one is more scared now that their family's security it's completely unknown? Which one has more emotion pumping through their body and mind?

On all of the above: It depends. The one that feels the most amount of emotion is the human one. If both the boy and the girl, the man and the woman, are human then the answer is all of them feel the most amount of emotion. This was a trick question. That shouldn't be a trick question. We should answer immediately - both.

I won't speak for other cultures but let's consider the American culture.

- Which human is given more permission to have emotions? Women.
- Which human is expected to have more emotions? Women.
- Which human is given less permission to have emotions? Men.
- Which human is expected to have fewer emotions? Men
- Which human it's called weak for having emotions? Both.
- Which human has the ability to turn off their emotions? Neither.
- Which human experiences depression and anxiety? Both.
- Which human experiences significant physical symptoms from suppressing their emotions? Both.
- Which human was trained on how to navigate and use their emotions in a healthy way? Neither.
- Which human feels ashamed when they have

emotions and feel like they can't handle them? Both.

- Which human comfortably expresses their emotions? Neither.
- Which human is seen as a badass for being able to feel their emotions and express them? Neither.
- Which human is seen as a badass for suppressing emotions? Both.
- Which human suffers the greatest consequences for not knowing how to navigate their emotions-- internal world?

Both men and women suffer immensely from not knowing how to navigate their internal world in a way that serves them at a higher level. Hopefully, as you read through these questions, you were able to see how crazy what's been happening really is. This idea that girls are weak and boys are strong is rapidly changing toward something far more accurate. Boys and girls are strong and what we really need to add to the conversation is boys and girls have every emotion and both need to learn how to navigate them.

For centuries, strength has been demonstrated through physical activity, force, and emotional suppression. It's completely illogical and isn't working. It's created a severe handicap on the human experience. The value of emotional intelligence has been on the rise slowly but surely since about 1990. However, human emotion still remains stigmatized in mainstream society. Because we are so physically focused, and validating only what we can touch and see, we have just had a terrible time wrapping our heads around the importance of the unseen and the untouchable.

Love, anger, joy, shame, peace, fear, excitement, jealousy, hope, sadness etc., these come up for us as human beings every day whether we choose to acknowledge them or not. The thing is they are unavoidable. There is something about unacknowledge and unexpressed emotion that causes the human body and mind to experience duress. Early heart attacks, anxiety, clinical depression, arthritis, our immune system in general tanks under stress. It's all interconnected. It's hard science today that the mind is completely interconnected with the body.

We love to simplify with straightforward cause-and-effect. "I hit my elbow on the table and now I have a bruise." Fantastic. Case closed, we made sense of it. "I am constantly exhausted. I am having trouble getting out of bed in the morning. Sometimes I have unexplainable anger and sadness." Fantastic. Pandora's box. Not sure if there's a quick answer or a quick pill. Maybe we could talk about our past for a couple of decades?

There's nothing wrong with talk therapy. It can really help. But there is something that's going to continue to be very wrong if we don't re-frame the value of emotions and the value of learning how to feel them without doing weird shit or breaking into an open sprint. This whole "women have emotions and men don't have emotions" has got to go if for no other reason than men are starting to truly break down and fall behind. It's not because they are weak and it's not because they've done something wrong.

It's because they are trained from a young age to be ashamed of an enormous aspect of how to successfully function.

I have a son and trying to help him build his emotional intelligence while he's surrounded by the ancient, outdated "boys don't cry" suppression model is difficult, to say the least. I want him to truly be happy throughout his life and a huge aspect of him being happy is knowing how to handle being sad without suppressing it. Men are trained from as young as birth to suppress emotion to fit into an outdated model of strength and then enter into a profound irony as they get older. As adults, they are accused of being insensitive, emotionally degenerate, and unable to show up for their partners and children in a way that's fulfilling for all parties involved, including themselves. This creates a stifled volcano of emotion. They feel disconnected, lonely, a sense of failure at lurking at every turn.

Many men only feel confident at work because it's the one place where they feel like they know what they're doing. A much-needed change of landscape is emerging with emotional intelligence growing in value inside of corporations and workplaces. Men are being left behind not knowing how to do something that they were told to never do if they wanted to be a real man. Many have very low emotional intelligence.

I refuse to not at least try to help for my son's sake and all of the boys and men and are spiraling off into a confusing but necessary shift. Balance is emerging. The balance of BOTH masculine and feminine energy inside all of us is fundamentally necessary for optimal human function.

Being a woman and experiencing a powerful shift in my own masculine and feminine energy moving towards balance has been remarkable. I cry when I see young girls and women showing up as the hero in a movie or in a story because I understand how powerful this is for both men and women. Women are slowly but surely showing up in their full potential with far less minimization of their value. It's truly amazing to be alive during this time. Experiencing history in the making.

If we don't become more conscious about how we got here, we could accidentally swing to the other end of the pendulum leaving men in a terrible position. We are all born as babies and then indoctrinated into our cultural norms by parents, family, teachers, peers, and media. We have to take responsibility for what we teach our babies about what it means to be a man or a woman. We need to take responsibility for teaching ourselves and our children how to become masters of our inner world. The next time we feel like shaming a child for expressing emotion when he or she is young and then shaming him or her for not expressing enough emotion or too much when as adults, let's stop and think about how we can do this differently as conscious humans.

The biggest battles I've ever fought and won were inside of myself. Gaining insight and courage to realize how powerful my emotions are and to not run has completely changed my life. It's been liberating and life-changing for me to know how to navigate them without needing to escape. Today, I have peace and strength that I had never known before... I have awakened a new kind of warrior within. A warrior that is strong enough to feel every part of being human with love and acceptance. I am no longer afraid. I'm the strongest I've ever been and one of my greatest victories to date: being strong enough to cry.

Feel
Your
Feelings

How have the stereotypes surrounding
gender and emotions
personally affected you?

_____

_____

_____

_____

_____

_____

_____

_____

_____

ABOUT THE AUTHOR

Erica Ormsby is a transformational keynote speaker, Bestselling author, and co-founder of Lighthouse Global Publishing & PR LLC. Her desire to powerfully and strategically get people excited and able to show up as they meant too is utterly contagious. Visit her online at ericainspired.com.